What Does Being

JEWISH

Mean?

*Read-aloud responses to questions
Jewish children ask about history, culture, and religion*

RABBI E. B. FREEDMAN,
JAN GREENBERG, AND
KAREN A. KATZ

A FIRESIDE BOOK
PUBLISHED BY SIMON & SCHUSTER
NEW YORK   LONDON   TORONTO   SYDNEY

FIRESIDE
Rockefeller Center
1230 Avenue of the Americas
New York, NY 10020

This Fireside edition 2003

FIRESIDE and colophon are registered trademarks
of Simon & Schuster, Inc.

For information about special discounts for bulk purchases,
please contact Simon & Schuster Special Sales at
1-800-456-6798 or business@simonandschuster.com

Book design by William Ruoto

Manufactured in the United States of America

3   5   7   9   10   8   6   4   2

Library of Congress Cataloging-in-Publication Data

Freedman, E. B.
What does being Jewish mean?/read-aloud responses to questions
Jewish children ask about history, culture, and religion/ by E. B.
Freedman, Jan Greenberg, and Karen A. Katz.
p.   cm.
Includes index.
Summary: Answers to questions commonly asked about the daily
practices and beliefs of Judaism.
1. Judaism—Miscellanea—Juvenile literature.   [1. Judaism—
Miscellanea.   2. Questions and answers.]   I. Greenberg, Jan.
II. Katz, Karen A.   III. Title.
BM51.F74   1991
296—dc20   90-46249

ISBN-13: 978-0-7432-5413-7
ISBN-10:   0-7432-5413-9

This book is dedicated to my dear wife Shaindy and my beautiful children: Moshe, Sarena, Minna, Shlomo, Elisheva, Shalom, and Shaya. I hope they will always love their Hebrew School education.
—Rabbi E. B. Freedman

For Rachel and Larry, with all my love.
For my father and stepmama, who are so dear to me.
And for my mother, who inspired me with a love of Judaism and whose beautiful memory I carry always in my heart.
—Jan Greenberg

For my family—Larry, my husband and best friend, and Mitchel and Steven, my precious sons.
For the Tintori and Katz families—to whom I am lucky enough to belong.
And for Jewish children everywhere who are not free to study their religion, in the hope that they will someday soon be able to study Torah.
—Karen A. Katz

Acknowledgments

On the first day of Shavuot 1990 (May 30, 6 Sivan 5750) I was called to the Torah as an adult Bat Mitzvah, following two years of intensive study with my friend Pamela David and thirteen other women from Congregation Shaarey Zedek, Southfield, Michigan. During the second year of the Bat Mitzvah class, this book became a reality, and work meetings with Rabbi Freedman became wonderful study sessions in their own right.

I have had many teachers of Torah, both by word and by example. I am grateful to them all. I would especially like to acknowledge my family, Rabbi Milton Arm, Rabbi Solomon Gruskin, and Geri Levit, who were my first teachers; Rabbi Irwin Groner and Rabbi William Gershon, for their exceptional abilities to teach, inspire, and guide; Rabbi Chuck Diamond, for making Hebrew School an adventure for our children; and the many friends both here and in Israel who are responsible for my Zionist education and activity.

Acknowledgments

And my special gratitude to Rae Sharfman—who suggested that Jan and I contact Rabbi Freedman to collaborate on this book.

—KAREN A. KATZ

Contents

Contents

What Does Being
JEWISH
Mean?

Foreword

We are the People of the Book, and until two generations ago most every Jewish child had the privilege of a formal Jewish education. Generally their parents were also well versed enough in the Jewish traditions to answer most of the questions that were posed to them by their children. Today, unfortunately, the links in the chain are not nearly that strong. Many parents who do have a strong Jewish identity and Jewish feelings still find themselves groping for the answers to some of the basic and fundamental questions about Yiddishkeit. Parents are often caught in a paradoxical situation. On one hand they try to lead a more Jewish lifestyle, feel enriched by Judaism, enjoy experiencing the holidays in their home, attempt to practice more of the rituals, and instill the same feeling in their children. But on the other hand, when their children ask why, parents are frustrated and cannot satisfy the youngsters' inquisitive minds.

When Karen and Jan approached me, looking to provide answers to the types of questions that their own children have asked them, they proposed this project. I immediately felt challenged and compelled to join them in working on this book, which we hope will help a broad audience.

The Torah is a living and exciting guide to life: It is as relevant to our urban, sophisticated children living in an age of harnessed solar energy as it was four thousand years ago to our young forefather Abraham, when he was searching for the higher source behind solar energy. I believe our Torah, our history, and our people's heritage can be as meaningful, vibrant, and exciting to our children as they were to our great-grandparents when they were children or, for that matter, as they were to the young budding Jewish scholars in Spain, Italy, Babylon, or Egypt. Yiddishkeit is like everything else we wish our children to get excited about. If we want them to enjoy it, we have to tease their interest and spark their curiosity. I hope you will find enough in this book to tease your child's interest and spark his or her curiosity so that he or she will want to go to Hebrew School and seek out the rich rewards that familiarity with Judaism brings.

There are many different streams of Judaism, and, of course, there are many different levels of commitment to the practice of the traditions. This book is not meant to impose a lifestyle.

As an Orthodox rabbi, I have tried to draw on my experience in working with children from diverse backgrounds from across the spectrum of Judaism. When answering the questions, I have attempted to convey universal appreciation for our traditions and a sense of the beauty of the traditional interpretation of the *mitzvot* of the Torah, veering away whenever possible from differences in opinions and dogmatic disputes.

It is not an *Halakic* guide or a book about the dos and don'ts of Judaism—it is a starter book for children who have come in contact with Jewish traditions and are curious about the whys behind the customs and practices they have seen being observed. I hope that some of the things they learn in this book will lead them to want to go to Hebrew School and send them on a lifelong quest and love affair with our Torah, our people, and our very rich heritage, which have helped us survive for more than five thousand years.

—RABBI E. B. FREEDMAN

Introduction

Art Linkletter proved that "kids say the darnedest things." Kids also ask the darnedest questions, particularly our bright, inquisitive Jewish children, who often pose knotty philosophical questions that leave parents stumped for quick and appropriate answers.

Why can't I see God?
Why doesn't God stop the suffering in the world?
Is everything in the Bible true?

Jewish parents want to give reasonable answers, but often they are not sure what the proper Jewish response is. For example, when a child asks, "Where do bad people go when they die?" many Jewish parents don't know if Hell is a concept within the framework of Judaism.

The seeds of this book were planted when our children began posing a continuous stream of incisive questions that we found challenging to answer. As two writers who happen to be friends, we found ourselves comparing notes about our children's questions and how we answered them. We decided that there ought to be a book dealing with the kinds of questions that come from the unique and often magical perspective of children. And who better to help us answer such questions than a rabbi, particularly one with as extensive a background in children's education as Rabbi E. B. Freedman. As director of Yeshivath Beth Yehudah, a Hebrew School and secular school attended by 630 children between the ages of four and eighteen, Rabbi Freedman has heard nearly every question imaginable about kids, God, and Judaism. When we met with him for the first time to discuss the project, there was an immediate agreement on the value of such a book and a sense of joy that we could make a contribution that would enrich Jewish children everywhere and serve as a tool for caring parents.

It is our hope that this book will provide children and their parents with a ready source of answers to perplexing questions in an easy-to-read, concise, question-and-answer format. The book is geared toward, but certainly not limited to, families with children between the ages of eight and thirteen. The answers are written in a language and tone understandable to children, making the book a useful reference guide for parents who want to brush up on their own knowledge or respond to their children without having to wade through more lengthy and complex volumes. Using this book, parents will not have to search for answers and then adapt them into simplified form.

In recent years there has been a resurgence of interest among young Jewish adults in the richness of their Jewish traditions and religion. Many who had only a passing knowledge of Judaism now find themselves as parents, wishing to reestablish a stronger link with their heritage. Adult bar and bat mitzvah classes are increasing in number, and Hebrew School enrollments are higher than ever, as parents seek to provide their children with a stronger Jewish education than they themselves might have had.

Nevertheless, children whose schedule is already jam-packed with homework; play; lessons in music, dance, and sports; and other after-school activities might very well ask, "Why do I have to go to Hebrew School?" With Rabbi Freedman's help and expertise, we answer this question and a host of others to help parents respond honestly and knowledgeably to their children.

These answers are generic in nature and applicable to Orthodox, Conservative, and Reform Jewish families. This book is a handy reference guide to some of the most common questions dealing with daily practice, customs, and beliefs. It is not meant to be an all-encompassing encyclopedia of Jewish knowledge and philosophy but rather an intriguing and informative response to some of the real questions that real kids ask. Organized into categories covering the various aspects of custom and belief, the format of the book makes it easy to zero in on a specific topic without wading through an excess of unrelated material.

It is our hope that this book will be a springboard for discussions between children and their parents, that it will spark a lifelong quest for meaningful answers, and that it will engender a better understanding of Judaism and a love for its teachings.

—JAN GREENBERG AND KAREN A. KATZ

What Does Being
JEWISH
Mean?

Jewish Ideas, Philosophies, Concepts, and Beliefs

1. What does God look like?
God doesn't look like anything specifically. God's presence is in everything, including each of us. However, His presence has no particular physical limitations or boundaries.

2. Why can't I see God?
God doesn't reveal Himself in one specific way. If He did, our minds and imaginations would be limited to that revelation. God wishes our hearts, minds, and souls to grow to greater and greater heights of perception and appreciation of Him without any limitations.

3. Why can't God talk to me?
He can, and He does. He has talked to all people through the Torah (the Bible), which has messages in it for every individual. And He talks to us through all kinds of experiences and events. We don't always realize that God is talking to us. We often make the mistake of thinking a

message from God was just a coincidental event or an accident.

4. Why does God let animals get hit by cars?

Seeing a pet get hurt is often the first exposure that a child has to misery in this world. Unfortunately, there is a great deal of misery and suffering in the world, and part of our job in growing up is learning how to cope with this misery, how to make it better if that is possible, and how to understand that God has a reason for everything that happens. Our religion teaches us that we must look for the good in the world and to do what we can to promote good and lessen misery.

One of our goals in life is to learn that God has a plan and that we must trust Him. God wants us to develop the ability to deal properly with misery.

When we see an injured animal and feel sad for it, we are becoming sensitive to the sufferings of animals and, in turn, of people—which will help us become caring people who will try to ease suffering in the world and make it a better place.

5. Why does God let people get sick and/or suffer?

There is not one single answer as to why people get sick or suffer. We must trust God and have faith that He has a reason for everything that happens in life. We must remember that, whatever happens, there is something to learn that will make us better people.

For example, if someone gets sick, the people around him who love him will be able to perform a great *mitzvah* (commandment or good deed) through helping, caring, and praying for that person. They can become better parents or children and more loving people because of this illness. Think of all the people who have gotten involved in hospital charities and other causes fighting illness because they have experienced their own or a loved one's pain during illness.

Furthermore, maybe this particular person's illness will help doctors find a cure for a disease or improve medical treatments. Maybe the person who is sick will have a chance to rethink his life and choose to dedicate himself to helping others.

Every seemingly bad event can cause many good things to happen. We don't know God's plan exactly and why at times people suffer, but we can make every painful experience an opportunity to make ourselves and the world around us better.

6. Why are there bad people in the world? Can't God stop them?

There are bad people in the world because everybody has a choice to be good or bad, and these people have chosen to be bad. God can stop them. Sometimes He chooses to, and sometimes He doesn't. There may be many bad people whom God chose to stop that we will never know about because they were never given the opportunity to carry out their evil intentions.

There can be many reasons why God doesn't stop some bad people. God sometimes may wish to teach lessons by using bad things that happen as examples. Sometimes things that seem bad turn out to be good in the long run. Sometimes sinners and bad people change their ways and become good. We know that God has a plan for everything. We don't always know the whole plan. We have faith and trust in God that the whole plan works out for the good.

7. Does God have feelings?

Human beings have feelings, and humans understand how other humans think and react. But God is not human and we do not understand everything about Him. So it is not possible for us to say for certain that God has feelings. Yet the Torah does refer to God with characteristics such as kindness, mercy, anger, forgiveness, and so forth. These are characteristics used to describe human feelings. The Torah speaks to us about God's behavior in terms that we can understand—human terms. It is telling us that some of our actions will bring out a specific response from God. For example, doing a *mitzvah* (good deed) will bring out God's merciful response. A sin will evoke reactions similar to human anger. That does not mean God has feelings like humans do. It means that there is a cause-and-effect relationship between our actions and God's responses.

God's mercy is infinitely more merciful than any human mercy. Yet we cannot describe it as "a feeling" in human terms because God is not human.

8. What does it mean that the Jews are the Chosen People?

Like the oldest child in a family, the captain of a sports

team, a commander in the army, or even the president of the United States, some people are chosen for great responsibility. They are usually asked to behave better and more responsibly than everybody else. The Jews were chosen by God in that way and given the Torah and *mitzvot*, which involve living up to special responsibilities.

9. What does God expect from the Jews?

There are many obligations that we have as Jews. Everything that is expected of us is stated in the Torah. We should study it as a sort of blueprint for our lives to make us better people. Some examples of these obligations are to be loving and kind, to be caring, to be ethical, and to be responsible citizens of the world.

10. Who made God? How could God always be?

There are some things that we as humans, no matter how smart we are or become, will never understand. They are beyond our ability to comprehend. God's existence always was and always will be. God wasn't created, He was always there. No matter how much we think about it, we will never really understand it. It is really a matter of faith.

11. Can God know my thoughts and everything I do?

Yes. God is all-knowing. That means God knows everything that has happened and everything that will happen.

12. What does *Messiah* mean?

Messiah comes from the Hebrew word *Mashiach*, which means "anointed." What does *anointed* mean? When a king is anointed, we pour oil on his head and pronounce him the anointed king. This was the old traditional way of crowning a king. So *Mashiach*, or Messiah, means "the anointed one." When we refer to the Messiah we are referring to a specific leader who will come at a specific time called the Messianic Era.

13. What is the Messianic Era?

There are many references in the Books of the Prophets, which is part of the Bible, and many more references in the Talmud to the Messianic Era. These references can be found particularly in the Book of Isaiah (from Prophets) and in the section called *Sanhedrin* from the Talmud. These passages state that a time will come when there will be one clear, anointed leader of the people of Israel, recognized not only by all Jews but by Gentiles (non-Jews) as well. This leader will be called the Messiah, the appointed one, and no one will dispute his universal appeal as the leader of all Jews.

He will be a man of great wisdom and great peace, and he will singlehandedly bring the world to an era of peace. Through his teachings, his actions, and his leadership the whole world will become a place of tranquility and peace.

14. When is the Messiah coming and how will we know for sure that he's here?

The Messiah will be such a clear and accepted leader and make such an impact on peace and tranquility in the world that we will all know that the Messianic Era has arrived. We will stop waging wars with each other. There will be no nuclear weapons and no longer any threat of a nuclear war.

There will be no more enemies among the different nations of the world.

We know this is what will happen because of the specific references in the Bible, particularly in the Book of Isaiah, that refer to the Messianic Era as a time when even natural enemies in the animal kingdom will coexist peacefully. One passage says "the wolf shall also dwell with the lamb, and the leopard shall lie down with the kid, and the calf and the young lions and the fatling together."* Another reference states that people shall "beat their swords into plowshares and their spears into pruning-hooks. Nation shall not lift up sword against nation, neither shall they learn war any more."**

Because of the these dramatic changes in the world, where for the first time there will be universal brotherhood and peace, it will be evident to everyone that the Messiah has come. There will be no doubt. His leadership will be accepted by everyone in the world without question.

15. Will other things be different in the Messianic Era?
The world will continue normally when the Messiah comes, except for the major difference that there will be total peace and goodwill in the world. Nothing miraculous will take place. Everyday life will go on much as we know it, except that there will be no more weapons and no more war, and the Jews will have one great leader, who is respected by everyone, Jew and non-Jew alike.

* Isaiah 11:6
** Isaiah 2:4

16. Will the Messiah have superpowers like the X-Men or Superman?

No. According to the interpretation of the Messianic Era by the great rabbi and scholar Moses Maimonides, who lived at the end of the twelfth century, the Messiah will not have any superhuman powers or abilities. He will not be able to fly, he will not have magnificent strength or anything like that. He will be a normal human being who exceeds the qualities of other people by so much that he will be accepted by all Jews and Gentiles as the clear leader of the Jews.

Some of you may have heard that when the Messiah comes, those who have died will come back to life and other amazing events will take place. There is a school of thought that teaches this; however, Maimonides states that nothing extraordinary will happen.

The only amazing thing is that there will be worldwide peace—which is a pretty spectacular thing in itself.

17. What are angels?

Angels are messengers of God. We often picture angels as somewhat human-looking forms with wings and halos, which is actually an artist's idea of what they might look like. This image became so popular that most people think of angels in this way. However, angels can look like anything or anyone that God chooses them to look like.

The first reference we have to angels in the Torah is when God sent three messengers to Abraham. The first angel was sent to visit and heal Abraham, who was sick. The second was sent to inform Abraham that even though he was elderly and he and his wife, Sarah, had never had children, their prayers would be answered and they would have a son. The third angel was sent by God to destroy the terribly evil cities of Sodom and Gomorrah, whose people refused to repent for their evil ways. The Bible said that these angels were dressed in the style of that period and appeared to Abraham as three regular wayfarers who were hungry and thirsty on a very hot day.

So angels are special messengers of God sent by Him to do specific tasks and can take on any shape or appearance that the mission calls for. Sometimes angels can be assigned to missions that are not that pleasant. For instance, when someone dies we say he was visited by "the Angel of Death," which means God decided that that person's time in this world was over and he sent a messenger to return his soul to his Maker.

18. What does it mean when we call somebody an angel?

To call someone an angel means that person has acted as if he or she were sent by God to do something good. For instance, when someone donates a major gift to a hospital or to another charity, we refer to him or her as an angel. Or when a child is behaving especially well, his or her mother may refer to that child as a little angel.

19. What is a soul?

The Hebrew word for "soul" is *neshama*. It is the spiritual essence of a physical person that each of us is born with, and it continues to exist after we die.

It is the sum of our personality, our thoughts, our emotions, and our feelings. According to Jewish tradition we are given a soul when we are born; our soul returns to God to be judged after we die.

Our duty in life is to do the best job we can and to do the right things so that when we return to God after our lifetime we come with a purer, better, and more spiritually developed soul than the one with which we were born.

20. Was Jesus Jewish?

Yes, he was. He was a Talmudic student and is mentioned in the Talmud. During his life he turned away from some of the practices of Judaism. After his death, his followers created a different religion, which became the basis for Christianity.

21. Why don't Jews believe in Jesus?

The Torah itself teaches us that no prophet or teacher can arise and change the laws of the Torah. Jesus and his followers attempted to change the laws of the Torah. Therefore, he cannot be considered a leader of the Jewish people.

22. Why don't we have Christmas trees?

A Christmas tree is a religious symbol of Christmas, which is a Christian religious holiday. Jews have an obligation to practice only their own religion and not to observe the customs and practices of other religions.

Celebrations of Life

23. Why are Jewish males circumcised?

Circumcision is a physical symbol of our devotion to God and of God's choosing us as His People. Since the time of Abraham, all Jewish males have been circumcised. It was part of Abraham's agreement with God, which is called the Covenant. Part of the symbolism is that we understand that a person is born incomplete, that people have to refine and improve themselves. That is our purpose in life. We should not be satisfied with our basic selves but should always strive to improve on our nature, to become better and more complete human beings.

In Hebrew, "circumcision" is called *Brit milah,* commonly referred to as a *bris. Brit* means "covenant"; *milah* means "circumcision." Together they mean "Covenant of the circumcision" and are used to refer to both the circumcision procedure and the ceremony.

A *bris* is a very joyous occasion, usually accompanied by a festive meal and blessings thanking God for the ability to perform this *mitzvah.* The procedure itself involves removing a layer of foreskin from the baby's penis. At this time the child is welcomed into the Jewish community and is given his Hebrew name.

24. Why do I have a Jewish name, and how are Jewish names chosen?

Even though we all have American, or English, names, it is still important that we have a Hebrew name as well and that we are proud of it. A Hebrew name is the name that we are given when we are born and is used for all the Jewish traditions: for our bar or bat mitzvah, for when we are called to the Torah, and on religious documents when we get married or divorced.

In addition, we use our Hebrew names to offer prayers when we are sick. Our Hebrew names are also written on our tombstones.

Having a Hebrew name is one way to express our pride in being Jewish, showing that we appreciate our thousands of years of heritage and all the wonderful things that Jews and the Jewish tradition have brought to the world.

Most Hebrew names come from the Bible, and they are an honor to have because they are remembrances of and references to heroic and great people. Knowing our Hebrew name, its translation, and where it comes from ties us to a rich tradition, which is thousands of years old. A Hebrew name is usually a name that many, many Jews have carried proudly before us. Most often, a child is given the same Hebrew name as a relative, to honor that person. Ashkenazic Jews (Jews whose ancestors came from Eastern European countries) customarily use only names of deceased relatives, whereas Sephardic Jews (Jews whose ancestors came from Mediterranean and Arabic countries) have the custom of using the Hebrew names of living relatives.

Studying the tradition of our own individual name can give us a great sense of history and belonging to our people. For instance, the name *Moshe* is the same name as the person to whom God gave the Torah at Mount Sinai more than three thousand years ago. It is the same name borne by Moses Maimonides, who lived some eight hundred years ago. He was a great teacher, writer, rabbi, medical doctor, and adviser to the sultan of Egypt. Moshe is also the name of a famous and popular Israeli soldier, Moshe Dayan, who was Israel's leading general during the Six-Day War in 1967. These are just three examples of some of the well-known men who were named Moshe. Every Hebrew name has an exciting history worth examining.

25. What is a *mitzvah*?

The translation of the word *mitzvah* is "commandment," referring to one of the 613 *mitzvot*, or commandments, in the Torah. It has also come to mean any good deed. For instance, when you do a kindness or favor or an act of charity, we say you did a *mitzvah*.

26. What is a bar or bat mitzvah?

Every Jewish child reaches an age of responsibility—for girls, it's their twelfth birthday, and for boys, it's their thirteenth birthday. On that day they are considered to be adults and, therefore, responsible for their own actions, according to Jewish law.

In Hebrew, the word *bat (bas)* means "daughter of" and the word *bar* means "son of." *Mitzvah,* of course, means "commandment." So the words combined mean "son or daughter of commandment." That means the young person has become obligated on his or her own to do the *mitzvot* (the commandments). The bar or bat mitzvah ceremonies, the calling to the Torah, the parties, all commemorate this coming of age. Until this point it was the parents' obligation to train the child or to see that a teacher trained the child about the Torah and *mitzvot.* Now that young person has reached the legal age to be responsible on his or her own. According to Jewish law, all the legal responsibilities that a person has in terms of ownership of property, legal documents, and being a witness (in Jewish legal matters) begin at the age of *mitzvah.*

For example, technically and legally, according to Jewish religious law, if a child does damage to property before his or her bar or bat mitzvah, it is the parents' responsibility to make restitution (payment). After the bar or bat mitzvah, the teenager becomes responsible for his or her own actions and must be the one to make restitution.

In addition, after the age of bar mitzvah, a boy is required to put on *tefillin.* After the age of bat mitzvah, a girl is required to pray daily.

Thus it is only after bar or bat mitzvah that a child gains the full responsibility of being a true member of the people of Israel in his or her own right.

27. What is Confirmation or Consecration?

Confirmation (or Consecration) is a ceremony in which

Jewish boys and girls express their devotion and commitment to Judaism. This ceremony usually follows studies that take place after bar or bat mitzvah age. (In years past, many girls had a Confirmation in place of bat mitzvah.) Most Confirmations are held on Shavuot, the holiday on which we celebrate God's giving the Torah to Moses. Boys and girls somewhere between the ages of thirteen and sixteen are usually confirmed as a group. Confirmation is more common in Reform and Conservative synagogues than in Orthodox ones.

28. Why do Jews get married under a *chuppah*?
Jewish weddings traditionally took place outdoors. God promised Abraham that his descendants would be as numerous as the stars in the sky. By marrying outdoors, "under the stars," we are reminded to fulfill our obligation as Jews to bring new Jewish lives into the world under the sanctity of marriage.

The reason we have a *chuppah,* or "canopy," between ourselves and the sky is that the canopy represents the new home the couple is creating together. The four corners of the *chuppah* represent the four walls of a home. Just as a building such as a home requires care in its construction, so does a marriage, and just as a structure is built with love and effort, as something to be treasured, so should a marriage.

29. What is a *ketubah*?
A *ketubah* is a document that explains the responsibilities that a husband and wife have to each other in marriage. A Jewish marriage involves many such responsibilities, which

are taken so seriously that we enter into a contract that spells them out clearly.

For example, a husband is obligated to feed, clothe, and cherish his wife, and she has the right to divorce him if he doesn't live up to these responsibilities. If this happens, he then has the responsibility to provide financial support for her. A wife is obligated to love and cherish her husband and to be loyal to him.

A *ketubah* is often ornately decorated by an artist and usually written by a scribe. It is read during the marriage ceremony so that these obligations are clearly spelled out as the wedding takes place.

30. Why do we break a glass at a Jewish wedding?

A Jewish wedding is probably one of the happiest events in the human life cycle. By Jewish law, a festive meal (a *seudah*) is required at a wedding. There is generally music and dancing, and in the days of the Talmud, even the greatest Talmudic rabbis and leaders would entertain by performing acrobatics, juggling, dancing, and reciting rhymes to add to the merriment of the occasion.

According to the Talmud, the greatest social obligation of any Jew is to partake in the joy of a bride and a groom at their wedding. This can be done by giving gifts, dancing, or in some other way participating in the wedding. There is even a tradition called *shevah berakhot* where for seven days following the wedding the couple is entertained with special dinners at which seven special blessings (the *shevah berakhot*) are recited to celebrate the marriage.

It is, therefore, clearly a *mitzvah* to take part in the abundant joy of a wedding. However, even at the happiest of times, we have a responsibility to realize that our joy cannot be complete until the Temple of Jerusalem is rebuilt and is restored to our people. During the wedding ceremony, the groom breaks a glass to serve as a reminder of our heartbreak over the destruction of the Temple, the loss of the Temple service, and the scattering of the Jewish people. Amid all of our joy we must still remember the sorrow of the Temple's destruction.

31. What other customs are part of a Jewish wedding ceremony?

A rabbi not only officiates at a Jewish wedding but also lends holiness to the occasion by reciting the seven traditional blessings on the bride and groom.

There must be two witnesses chosen by the bride and groom. The witnesses must be Jewish, male, older than thirteen years of age, and must not be relatives of the bride or groom.

In addition, because the marriage is a legal matter, the groom must give the bride a ring as part of the transaction.

Death

32. Where do we go after we die?

Jewish tradition teaches that there is no physical but only a spiritual world after we die. Although our physical body "turns to dust" when we are buried in the ground, our soul (*neshama*) lives on forever. Our soul does not have a physical dimension to it. It is spiritual, so we as physical people don't really know or understand where it goes. We usually refer to where we go after life as "going to heaven."

33. Do we believe in reward for righteousness and punishment for evil after death?

Yes, but because there is no physical world after death our reward and our punishment do not come in a physical sense. Our reward is in the purest form of pleasure, a spiritual intimacy and closeness with God. In the same way, our punishment is a spiritual one, too. If we don't act properly during our lifetime, our soul will be punished after death by a distance and detachment from God.

34. Will I have to see bad people in heaven?

We don't have an absolutely clear picture of what heaven is like because the reward or punishment that will come to us in the next world is not necessarily physical but spiritual. If we do see people in heaven, we do not know what form they will take. Because we do not know much about what heaven is like, we should not spend too much time thinking about it but should use our energies to make our lives worthwhile, and when the time comes, we will know and understand about heaven.

We do know that we will be closer to God in heaven, and so we can conclude that no harm can come to us and we will know safety and peace.

35. Do Jews believe in the devil?

The usual perception of a devil is based on artists' conceptions of a being with horns, a red body, a tail, and a pitchfork. Jewish religion has no references to a devil like that. But the Jewish religion does have many references to forces of evil, often called in Hebrew *satan* or *yetzer harah,* "the evil inclination." Just as we recognize that angels are messengers of God and forces of good, we also recognize that evil forces in the world do exist and are messengers of temptation to do evil. However, Jews do not believe that these evil forces have a physical form such as the generally accepted image of a devil.

36. What is *Yizkor?*

Yizkor means "to remember." It is a special prayer or service that is said by relatives to remember a loved one who has died. The prayer is recited in a very solemn atmosphere in the synagogue on certain special occasions during the Jewish calendar year.

It is recited during services on the holidays of Yom Kippur, Passover, Sukkot, and Shavuot. *Yizkor* is said by children, parents, or spouses who have lost their relatives. The ark is opened during the service, and the prayers are said in the presence of the Torah scrolls. The loved ones and relatives not only offer prayers as part of the services; they also pledge charity. One of the best ways of commemorating or remembering someone who has died is to give charity to honor his or her memory so that good deeds continue to be done in his or her name. Even though the person who died can no longer do good deeds in this world, good deeds are still being done in his or her honor.

37. What is *Kaddish,* and why do only mourners recite it?

Kaddish is a communal prayer praising God and His name. It is recited in public with a *minyan*. It is one of our oldest prayers and is written in Aramaic, an ancient biblical language.

Someone mourning a close relative who has recently died is given the honor of reciting *Kaddish*. Because God is more sensitive to a mourner, we feel He will listen more closely and sympathetically to a prayer offered by the mourner on behalf of the community. Also, at a time when a mourner might feel forlorn and alone, the honor of reciting *Kaddish* is a way of drawing that person back into the community, giving him or her a sense of purpose and comfort and guiding him or her away from despair and toward a rededication to life and to God. By saying *Kaddish* a Jew says "although life is hard for me, I still believe in the values of life."

While *Yizkor* specifically recalls the deceased loved one and honors his or her memory, *Kaddish* makes no mention of death or of any individual person. It is simply a prayer of praise to God, reaffirming our trust and faith in Him.

38. What is *yahrzeit*?

Yahrzeit is the anniversary of the day of someone's death. It is figured according to the Jewish calendar.

39. What is a *yahrzeit* candle, and why do we light it?

A *yahrzeit* candle is a candle that lasts for at least twenty-four hours, and we light it on the *yahrzeit* of a loved one. Some people also light a *yahrzeit* candle on the special days that *Yizkor* is said.

Light is intangible. It cannot be felt. It also dispels darkness. So, too, does the memory of a loved one. To honor and memorialize people who have died and to remind us of the souls of those who are no longer with us, we light *yahrzeit* candles. We trust that their souls live on and that the goodness of the deeds they have done during their lifetime will continue to dispel darkness and light up our world.

40. Why do we wash our hands when we leave a cemetery?

There are many laws and traditions in the Torah about how to maintain spiritual purity and what to do when exposed to impurities. These laws are very complicated and detailed, and many of them only apply to a time when the Temple is operating in Jerusalem. Because we do not have a Temple today, these laws and traditions are not known to many people. However, one of these traditions—the custom of washing our hands when we leave a cemetery—is still widely practiced.

After being exposed to certain kinds of impurities, such as the remains of a dead person, it is proper to wash the hands. Although the Torah has many laws that place great emphasis on health and physical cleanliness, this is a custom that has nothing to do with personal hygiene. It is simply a matter of keeping ourselves *spiritually* pure and a way of maintaining a separation between the living and the dead.

The Bible—Its Stories and People

41. Is everything in the Bible true?

According to traditional belief, everything that is written in the Bible—even the miracles—is true. Almost every miracle that is recorded in the Bible was witnessed by thousands of people. They were public events, which occurred not in the sight of just a few individuals but in the presence of enormous numbers of people. Some examples of these miracles are the Jews' going out of Egypt, the splitting of the sea, and the giving of the Ten Commandments. Most of the miracles that were recorded in the Bible were written down at the time they happened, so that they wouldn't be exaggerated and thought of as only a legend.

42. Why don't the kinds of miracles in the Bible happen today?

Many things that happen in our time can be considered miracles. The founding of the State of Israel and the rebuilding of our people immediately after the Holocaust in 1948 could be considered a miracle.

In 1967, the State of Israel was in great danger. Israel was surrounded by five hostile nations determined to destroy her. Israel was saved in only six days, and the air forces and armies of the other countries were destroyed. That war is known as the Six-Day War. Many military experts, rabbis, and laymen believe that the Six-Day War was a miracle.

Even in biblical times we weren't saved from every dangerous situation by a miracle. God chooses when to use a miracle. Once again, we don't understand everything He does because we're not as smart as He is. But we do see again and again throughout history that God often chooses to save us through miracles. Over thousands of years the Jewish people were never entirely destroyed, even though there have been many enemies who tried to wipe us out. That in itself could be called a miracle.

43. Are there different kinds of miracles?

Yes. Because God created the world and controls everything in it, He can also change nature and make the world work differently when He wants to do so. That is one kind of miracle. The best example of this kind of miracle is when the Jews were freed from slavery in the land of Egypt. They were being pursued by their captors, the Egyptians. They came to the Red Sea. They didn't have any boats and couldn't go around the sea. Just as they were about to be recaptured by the Egyptians, God parted the waters of the Red Sea, and all the hundreds of thousands of Jews walked through the middle of the sea on dry land.

There are also other kinds of miracles that don't change

nature. They happen every day, but we don't necessarily understand them as miracles because we see them so often and take them for granted. Examples of this kind of miracle are the complexity of the human body, especially the brain, and also childbirth, with all its wonders. If a little child who lived a hundred years ago were to appear in our world today, look around, and see cars, computers, airplanes, televisions, cell phones, and Disney World, wouldn't he or she think all these wonders were miracles? The miracle of nature and our ability to understand it and to harness it to improve our lives could very well be God's greatest miracle—even greater than the splitting of the Red Sea.

44. Who wrote the Bible?

According to tradition, the Torah (or the Bible) was written down by Moses exactly as it was told to him by God on Mount Sinai some thirty-three hundred years ago. That is why the Bible is often referred to as the Five Books of Moses. However, the last few passages, which describe Moses' death, were written by his student Joshua.

45. Why do we kiss the Torah?

We kiss the Torah and other holy objects to show our respect, reverence, and love for them. In addition to the Torah we also kiss *tefillin*, *mezuzot*, prayer books, and other sacred items.

We usually kiss them when we first come in contact with them. We also kiss them if by accident they fall on the floor or become dishonored in some way.

46. What is the Talmud?

The Talmud is a collection of scholarly writings that was compiled by hundreds of Jewish sages (wise men). It was completed about fifteen hundred years ago and took four hundred years to write. It is the main body of Jewish religious writings and includes sixty-three *tractates* (volumes) of Jewish law, history, philosophy, moral teachings, and legends. The Talmud contains the Mishnah (laws) and the Gemara (explanation of and commentaries on the laws).

47. What is the Mishnah?

The Mishnah is a sort of encyclopedia of Jewish laws based on the Bible. It was compiled over a two-hundred-year period some two thousand years ago. It contains the thoughts, teachings, and philosophies of the leading scholars and rabbis of that time. It was the foundation on which the commentaries of the Talmud were written and is still studied today as the cornerstone of any program of intensive Jewish study. Some of the most famous scholars of Jewish tradition, such as the great Hillel and Rabbi Akiva, are quoted in the Mishnah.

48. What is the *Haftarah?*

The *Haftarah* is a very interesting concept. Each week in the synagogue a portion of the Torah (the Five Books of Moses) is read from the Torah scroll. We do that so that each of us can become more learned and familiar with the Bible. About two thousand years ago, most of the Jewish people lived under the Roman Empire. The Romans wanted to destroy the Jewish religion and culture and force all Jews to conduct themselves as Romans. The most significant thing they did in their attempt to destroy our religion was to ban the public reading of the Torah each week at the synagogue. They were convinced that that way the Jews would forget the Torah. But they were wrong.

The Jews got together, and instead of reading from the Torah, they read portions of the Books of the Prophets, which are holy books for the Jews that were not banned by the Romans. In choosing which portions to read each week, they chose sections of the Books of the Prophets that were similar in nature to those that would have been read from the Torah.

For instance, on the week that the story of Jacob's death and his stirring blessing to his children was to be read from the Torah, the Roman Jews read the story of King David's death and his blessing to his son, King Solomon, instead.

Now that we are free to practice our religion as we choose, we continue to read the *Haftarah* in the synagogue for two reasons. First, so that we always remember that there were many times when Jews were not free to read the Torah whenever they wished, and, second, to remind ourselves that there are many holy works besides the Five Books of Moses and that we should study those too.

49. There seem to be so many different ways of referring to the Bible that I get confused. What do all these words mean: *Torah, Bible, Five Books of Moses, Chumash, Tanach, The Ten Commandments,* and *Oral Law*?

TORAH. There is a broad usage for the word *Torah* and a narrow usage. In the broadest sense, *Torah* refers to any form of Jewish religious teaching. This could include anything from the Five Books of Moses to the writings of a contemporary, modern-day religious scholar. When someone says he is studying *Torah* he may be referring to Jewish philosophy, ethics, the Bible, or history. The word *Torah* actually means "teachings." In the more narrow usage, the word *Torah* refers to the first five books of the Bible, which are called the Five Books of Moses.

The Five Books of Moses are written on parchment by a religious scribe called a *sofer* and bound in a scroll. This scroll is called a Torah. Each Shabbat and holiday, during services, the Torah is taken out from its ornamental ark in the synagogue and a portion of the Torah is read by a person called the cantor. That part of the service is called the Torah reading.

THE FIVE BOOKS OF MOSES. The Five Books of Moses are the first five of twenty-four books of the Bible, or the "Written Law." These books were given to Moses by God on Mount Sinai. The five books cover twenty-five hundred years of the history of the Jewish people from the time of creation to the year 2448 of the Jewish calendar when the Jews entered Israel for the first time. The five books are:

Genesis (*Bereshit*), or "In the Beginning," which deals with
  creation until the Jewish people went down to Egypt;
Exodus (*Shemot*), which deals with the exodus of the Jews
  from Egypt;

Leviticus (*Vayikra*), which focuses on the laws pertaining to
the Temple and the land of Israel;

Numbers (*Bemidbar*), which relates the Jews' forty years of
wandering in the Sinai Desert;

Deuteronomy (*Devarim*), which is for the most part a review
of the first four books and includes Moses' blessing for the
Jews as they went into the land of Israel.

Throughout the entire Torah there are 613 commandments, or *mitzvot*, which instruct a Jew how to conduct his
or her daily life.

CHUMASH. The word *chumash* means "five" and is the Hebrew word that refers to the Five Books of Moses.

TANACH. The word *Tanach* is an acronym made up of three
Hebrew letters: *tav, nun, chaf. Tav* stands for Torah, *nun* for
Niviim (the Books of the Prophets), and *chaf* for *Ketuvim*
(Writings and Psalms). These are the three sections of the
Bible. Together these letters are read as *"Tanach"*—the He-
brew word for the Bible. The Bible is also referred to as the
"Old Testament" and the "Written Law."

The reason it is called the Old Testament is to distinguish
it from the New Testament, which is included in Christianity's version of the Bible.

The reason it is called the Written Law is because originally the twenty-four books of the Jewish Bible were the only
Jewish books that the rabbis permitted to be written. They
were written by the prophets of Israel, of whom Moses was
the first, and they were considered divinely inspired.

The explanation and interpretation of these works are considered the Oral Law, or the part of the Torah that was passed down through telling and retelling from generation to generation by the prophets and rabbis but never written down.

THE TEN COMMANDMENTS. The Ten Commandments were the first series of commandments, or *mitzvot*, that were given to Moses in front of all the people of Israel at Mount Sinai. This giving of the Ten Commandments was called "the Revelation." The Ten Commandments are part of the 613 commandments and were inscribed by God himself on two tablets. The Ten Commandments and the tablets have become symbols of Judaism found on synagogues, jewelry, and Jewish artifacts throughout the world. The story of the Revelation is recorded in the Second Book of Moses, or Exodus.

ORAL LAW. The Oral Law is the complete body of explanations and interpretations of the Bible or the Written Law. The Bible cannot be properly understood without these interpretations. The reason it is called the Oral Law is because originally these interpretations and explanations were given to Moses by God and told to the people by Moses in his generation and in each succeeding generation by the leading prophets, teachers, and rabbis. As the Jews began to spread out into many foreign nations these teachings began to get confused, so it became necessary to write down the teachings for future generations.

The Written Law encompasses two basic forms of teaching—the *Halakah*, which means "laws," and the *Aggadah*, which are the moral, ethical, and philosophical meanings behind the words of the Bible. Most of the ethical, philosophical, and moral teachings were written down in the body of work called the Midrash. The legal aspects were written down in the Mishnah. This writing took place about one thousand years after the Torah was given at Sinai. About four hundred years later, the Talmud was written; it is a much more elaborate series of books that combines a detailed look at the Midrash and the Mishnah. The Talmud is also commonly referred to as the Gemara. Gemara means "to learn."

MIDRASH. The Midrash is a collection of lore and legend written by sages (wise rabbis) from the time of the Talmud. The Midrash sheds light and wisdom on Jewish traditions. Some, but not all, *midrashim* appear in the Talmud.

50. What does *Halakah* mean?
Halakah is the word used for "Jewish law." The English translation of the word means "ways"—or the way we should live. The Jewish law process uses the Torah as a source and has been developed over thousands of years. The main body of codification (listing) of Jewish law is the *Shulchan Aruch*. It was compiled by Rabbi Joseph Karo in 1565 C.E. (the Common Era), and all contemporary Jewish *Halakic* works use the *Shulchan Aruch* as the basic source.

51. What is the first commandment in the Torah?
The first commandment is to be fruitful and to multiply.

The Talmud says that God, a mother, and a father are part-
ners in the creation of a new human being. In this way, God
has made men and women powerful, by giving them the
ability to help create new life.

God created all the things in the world for people to use
and enjoy. All of these things in the world would be useless
without people in the world; therefore, it is our responsibility to see that there are always people to enjoy the world
God has created.

52. Why weren't Adam and Eve Jewish?
According to the Bible, Adam and Eve were the first two humans created by God. The Jewish religion didn't start until
the time of Abraham (about two thousand years later)
when, through his own intelligence, Abraham discovered
the existence of God and decided to follow the ways of God.

53. Who was the first Jew?
Abraham was the first Jew. He lived about thirty-seven hundred years ago. His father and most of the people who lived
during that time were idol worshipers who served many
different gods and powers. Abraham was the first to realize
that to serve many gods made out of wood and stone was
not reasonable. He searched and he sought and he discovered that there was only one God in this world, and he
chose to serve Him. Serving one God is called monothe-
ism. Abraham was the first person in recorded history to be
monotheistic, which is why Judaism, Christianity, and Islam
all honor Abraham.

54. What is the Covenant that God made with Abraham?

A covenant is a solemn, binding agreement. When Abraham became the father of the Jewish people, God made a covenant with him. He promised Abraham that his offspring would be as numerous as the stars in the sky and the sands of the seashore. God also promised that the land of Israel would belong to the Jewish people. To remind all the future generations of Jews of the Covenant, all Jewish males have been circumcised from that time on. The act of circumcision is a symbol of the Covenant between God and Abraham.

55. Why did we have a king in the time of the Bible and not now?

At the early stages of our people's development, while all the Jews were settled in the land of Israel, there was a period of about five hundred years during which we had the relative tranquility and unity needed to appoint kings. Kings were our supreme leaders at that time, and some of our greatest historical personalities—such as Solomon and David—were kings.

The kings were appointed by the seventy members of the *Sanhedrin,* which was the judicial, legislative, and religious leadership council of the people of Israel.

Because we do not all live in Israel together, and we do not have the unified leadership of a *Sanhedrin,* and unfortunately have not lived in tranquility during the long period of the Diaspora, we do not have the good fortune of having a Jewish king today.

56. What are the Ten Commandments?

The Ten Commandments are the series of *mitzvot* (commandments) that were given to Moses by God on Mount Sinai. They are so important and fundamental that we accept them as the basis for living a just and moral life.

The Ten Commandments are:

1. Believe in God;
2. Do not serve idols;
3. Do not swear or use God's name for meaningless or false reasons;
4. Observe the Sabbath as a day of rest;
5. Respect and honor your parents;
6. Do not kill or cause bloodshed;
7. Be faithful to your husband or wife;
8. Do not steal;
9. Do not lie or falsify;
10. Do not be jealous of other people's possessions.

57. Who were our forefathers and foremothers?

Our forefathers were the famous leaders of the Jewish nation who followed in Abraham's footsteps. They were the earliest shapers and molders of our people. First there was Abraham and his wife, Sarah. Then came their son Isaac and his wife, Rebecca. Their son Jacob was the next leader, with his two wives, Rachel and Leah. They were called our forefathers and foremothers because they were the physical and spiritual originators of the Jewish people and we are their descendants. The stories of their lifetime are told in the first book of the Bible, called Genesis, or *Bereshit*.

58. What are the Twelve Tribes of Israel?

The Twelve Tribes of Israel were headed by the twelve sons and grandsons of Jacob, our forefather, and his wives. Each of Jacob's sons was the head of his own tribe, which lived in its own area within the land of Israel. The names of the sons (and their tribes) were Rueben, Simeon, Levi, Judah, Yissachar, Dan, Naphtali, Gad, Asher, Joseph (Ephraim and Menasseh), and Benjamin. Ten of the tribes were exiled. The remaining Jews today are identified as descendants of the tribes of Judah and Benjamin.

59. What is the difference between Kohen, Levi, and Yisrael?

A Jew who is considered a *Kohen* is a descendant of Aaron (Moses' brother), the first priest. In the days of the Temple, the priests were responsible for the ceremonies of worship that took place in the Temple, such as conducting services, offering sacrifices, burning incense, gift offerings, and so on. These priestly duties were passed on from one generation to another among Aaron's descendants. They had an obligation to keep themselves pure and on a high religious level.

In every generation there was one chief Kohen, called the "Kohen Gadol," who was the high priest and conducted the services in the Temple on Yom Kippur, which is the holiest service. He alone was allowed to enter the Holy of Holies, which was the holiest spot in the Temple, entered only on Yom Kippur. Even today, descendants of the family of Kohen, because they were chosen and ordained as the priestly representatives of the Jewish people, have certain restrictions involving whom they can marry and certain other matters.

A Jew who is a Levi is a descendant of Jacob's son Levi and his tribe. The Levites were on a religious level right below the Kohanim (plural of Kohen). The tribe of Levi sang in the Temple and served as the clergy. They were rabbis and religious leaders and also performed circumcisions and slaughtered animals for food according to the laws of *kashrut*. They were a family known for scholarship and leadership.

All other Jews are considered Yisrael (Israel). When Jews in the synagogue are called up to read the Torah, Kohanim are always called first, followed by Levites, and then by Yisrael.

Israel—Its People and Language

60. Why is Israel considered the Promised Land?

Since the time of Abraham the land of Israel has been considered the homeland of the Jewish people. God promised that this land (Israel) would be given to the children of Israel—which is why it is often called the Promised Land. From the time the Jewish people came out of Egypt, received the Torah, and became a nation, the greatest developments in Jewish history occurred in Israel. Many of our greatest kings, prophets, teachers, and sages lived and taught there. Almost all of the stories in the Bible occurred there, and our two Temples stood there.

Through the ages, many enemies of the Jews have tried to conquer us and take away our land. Many times we were driven out, and many times our people fought back valiantly to protect it. But throughout history and despite seemingly insurmountable trials and tribulations, we have always been able to keep a presence in the land that God promised us.

61. What does Diaspora mean?

The word *Diaspora* comes from the word *disperse*—which means "to scatter or spread widely." Jews who live in communities outside of Israel are considered to be living in the Diaspora.

62. What is a Jewish star?

The Jewish star, or Shield of David (as it is often called) is an ornamental and universally recognized symbol of Judaism. Some say each of its six corners represents a single day in God's creation of the world, with the center representing the Sabbath.

63. What is Zionism?

Zionism today is the name of the Jewish nationalistic movement that supports the establishment of a Jewish state. It is an organized effort to promote loyalty and devotion to Israel. The modern Zionist movement first made Jews all over the world aware of the need for a homeland and then brought them together to work toward this goal. Zionism represents a worldwide body of people, including Jews from all countries of the world, dedicated to a belief in the importance of Israel as the Jewish state—a homeland for all Jews.

Zionism is not new, though. Ever since the Jews were first forced by the Babylonians to leave the land of Israel as slaves, there has been a yearning to return. Throughout the ages of the Diaspora the land of Israel has been foremost in the minds and hearts of Jews all over the world.

This longing to return to their national homeland brought about the formation of a Zionist movement in the late 1800s. Theodor Herzl founded this movement, and in 1897 the first Zionist World Congress was held.

In June 1968, at the twenty-seventh Zionist World Congress in Jerusalem, the aims of Zionism were adopted as the "Jerusalem Program." These aims are:

The unity of the Jewish people and the centrality of Israel in Jewish life;

The ingathering of the Jewish people from around the world to their historic homeland;

Strengthening of the State of Israel;

The preservation of the identity of the Jewish people through the fostering of Jewish and Hebrew education and of Jewish spiritual and cultural values;

The protection of Jewish rights everywhere.

64. Why is Israel the Jewish homeland?

Since 1948, when Israel became a state, it has become a homeland for Jewish refugees from around the world. In fact, the Israeli government gives automatic citizenship to any person who is a Jew and wishes to live in Israel, regardless of what country he or she was born in or where he or she is living.

Even before 1948, survivors of the Holocaust in Europe began streaming into the Jewish homeland, and since then there have been influxes of Jews from almost every part of the world. Often escaping tyranny and persecution, they have come from such places as Hungary, Iran, Morocco, Syria, South America, South Africa, Eastern Europe, Ethiopia, and Yemen.

Since the early 1990s, we have seen the biggest wave of

immigration ever to take place, as Jews have arrived in Israel from Russia and Ethiopia. Hundreds of thousands of Soviet Jews made Israel their home after restrictions in Communist Russia were lifted and they were given permission to leave. Israel has also rescued many Ethiopians, airlifting them to new lives in Israel. Many Argentinean Jews are also fleeing to Israel to escape hardship and persecution.

65. Why is Israel so important to the Jewish people?

A great rabbi, the Vilna Gaon, once said that for the Jewish people Israel is a spiritually fertile land. Just as fruit grows better and in greater abundance on fertile soil, so too is Israel a healthy and spiritually fertile place for Jews to live.

Many of our greatest teachers and writings have come from Israel. Our greatest leaders have lived and subsequently died in Israel. In addition, some of our holiest places, like the burial places of our forefathers and the remains of our holy Temple, are in Israel. Likewise, many places in Israel are famous because the stories in our Bible took place there. Almost every city in Israel has hundreds of pages of Jewish history written about it.

Even today, Israel is filled with the best Jewish universities, *yeshivot*, scientific research centers, hospitals, and museums.

For Jews, Israel is the center of the world.

66. Why don't all Jews live in Israel now?

The long period of Diaspora and the complex forces of history have created countless Jewish communities around the world. It would be almost impossible for all of these communities to pick up entirely and move to Israel. Even if this were possible, Israel is a relatively small country and it couldn't absorb all Jews into its borders at one time.

In addition, each of us has his or her own personal reasons for choosing to live in Israel or not. Often our reasons are based on our jobs, our family relationships, or the roles we play in greater society. But every Jew should do what he or she can to help Israel even if he or she chooses to remain in the Diaspora. We can each help by financially supporting the country and its institutions or by visiting Israel and morally supporting it through tourism. Businesspeople and citizens of other countries can also offer political support to Israel through their own government systems. Most important, we must all remember that we have an obligation to Israel because it is our Promised Land and a homeland for all Jews who wish to live there.

67. Why have the Arabs fought so many wars with Israel?

The Arabs believe that the Jewish State of Israel was created at their expense. Regardless of our biblical claims and other reasons for retaining Israel as our homeland, they feel we do not have a right to the land.

Since 1948, there have been four different wars with Arab states—in 1948, 1956, 1967, and 1973. These battles were primarily territorial wars with the neighboring states of Egypt, Syria, Lebanon, Iraq, Saudi Arabia, and Transjordan (Jordan), which have never accepted Israel's claims to statehood.

In each war, Arab forces attacked Israel first, but Israel's tiny defense forces won out against a much larger enemy.

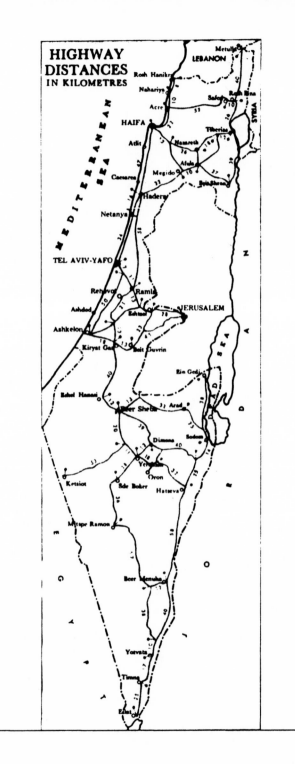

Of all of these countries, Egypt is the only one to sign a formal peace treaty with Israel.

68. Who are the Palestinians, and why are they fighting the Jews?

Palestinians are Arabs who claim to have been displaced by Israel when the country was created in 1948. They claim that they and their ancestors were not treated fairly when Israel was reestablished.

Most Palestinians live in the West Bank or the Gaza Strip. The West Bank is a narrow strip of land along the Jordan River. This area is also known by its biblical names of Judea and Samaria. The Gaza Strip is an area along the Mediterranean near Egypt.

69. What is the *intifada?*

The first *intifada* was a political movement that began in 1988 consisting of ongoing violent demonstrations and a series of strikes organized by Palestinians in the West Bank and Gaza Strip. Their constant upheavals were designed to convince the world that the Palestinians are treated unfairly by Israel and its government. The second *intifada*, started in the fall of 2000, is characterized by terrorist attacks against Israeli citizens by homicide bombers.

70. What is the PLO?

PLO stands for the Palestine Liberation Organization, which, as its name implies, was created to "liberate Palestine." It is headed by Yasir Arafat.

The PLO is a loosely formed organization with a history

of worldwide terrorism whose stated purpose has been to "drive Israel into the sea" and to reclaim the land that they maintain belongs to the Palestinians.

71. What is the Temple in Israel that we refer to, and what happened to it?

There were actually two temples in Israel. They were both destroyed.

The First Temple was built in Jerusalem by King Solomon. It stood for five hundred years and was destroyed by the Babylonians in 586 B.C.E. (before the Common Era). This was the first time that Jews were dispersed (scattered) from their homeland and the beginning of the Diaspora.

Seventy years passed before the Jews were allowed to return to the land of Israel and rebuild the Temple. The Romans destroyed the Second Temple nearly two thousand years ago, in about C.E. 70. In those days, Jerusalem was the capital for all Jews and the Temple was our holiest site. When the Temple was still standing, the Jews were in their greatest glory. There was a great and impressive service to God that took place in the Temple, and it was the source of inspiration to all Jewish people.

Three times a year the Temple was the gathering place of Jews from throughout the land. Men, women, and children gathered to witness very elaborate services marking the holidays of Sukkot, Pesach, and Shavuot. The Temple menorah was lit, incense was offered to God, sacrificial offerings were made, and the atmosphere was charged with devotion and festivity.

On the solemn holiday of Yom Kippur, the high priest

entered the most sacred area of the Temple, the Holy of Holies, to offer prayers of atonement for all the Jews.

It was a special commandment for all Jews to be present in the Temple for these holidays.

It was from the Temple that the seventy elders of the Jews, called the *Sanhedrin*, presided over the government. There the priest conducted the religious ceremonies for all the people. The Temple was the center of Jewish life.

But since the Romans destroyed the Temple, Jewish spiritual life has never really been able to recapture the intensity that it had achieved in those days.

According to the Mishnah, the First and Second Temples were both destroyed on the same day—the ninth day of the Hebrew month of *Av.* This day is referred to as *Tisha B'Av*, which is the annual day of national mourning for the Jews and is commemorated each year.

The three weeks before the ninth day of *Av* are also marked as a mourning period because during these three weeks many events happened that led up to the actual burning of the Second Temple. During this time the Romans encircled Jerusalem, pierced the walls of the Holy City, and gained their foothold there, making it possible for them to conquer and burn the city and carry its inhabitants off as slaves.

72. What is the Western Wall?

The Western Wall (or the *Kotel*) is the one wall of the Temple courtyard that was never destroyed. It stands in Jerusalem as a reminder to us of the glory that the Jewish people once had and that we hope to attain once again. It is our holiest shrine. It is also called the Wailing Wall because of the hundreds of generations who have turned to it with tears in their eyes and who have prayed for the rebuilding of the Temple.

Since 1967 the Wall is once again in the hands of Jews, under the control of the Israeli government. Since then, hundreds of thousands of Jews have flocked to see it, to touch it, and to pray in front of it. We consider our generation to be very fortunate to be able to stand in front of it and offer our prayers to God. Other generations weren't so fortunate, because for many years the Western Wall was under foreign control and we as Jews were not allowed to visit it.

73. Why do people put notes in the Western Wall, and what happens to the notes?

The site of the Temple is the holiest place for Jews, and the Western Wall is the one remnant of the Temple that for nearly two thousand years has never been destroyed. It has become the symbol of the holiest place in the world for Jews. We pray facing the direction of the Western Wall, and all synagogues in the world have been constructed in a way to make this possible.

The Western Wall is a place where Jews go to offer their special prayers. When Jews visit the Wall, they write their prayers on little slips of paper and tuck them into the crevices of the Wall with the fervent hope that God will answer them. Twice a year these notes are cleaned out of the Wall and buried with all the respect and love that is shown to religious articles.

74. Why do I need to learn to read, write, and speak Hebrew?

Hebrew is and always has been the universal language of Jews. Because we have had such a long Diaspora and have lived in many countries throughout the world, maintaining this universal language has been very important.

Hebrew is our language of prayer and study, and all of our religious teachings have been passed down to us in this language. Knowledge of Hebrew allows us to study the Bible, the Talmud, and other holy books in their original form, without having to depend on translations, which could change the meanings of certain words. Jews all over the world have been able to study the same ancient materials throughout our history because of this common language.

Also, if we didn't have a universal language, we would never be able to get together and communicate with each other. Because we have Hebrew, a Jewish person from Japan and one from the United States and one from Spain could all meet together in Israel and speak to each other in a common tongue.

75. Why do Jews pray together in Hebrew?

Because Hebrew is our universal language, praying in Hebrew is another way of keeping a bond between all Jewish people everywhere. By praying and studying in Hebrew we ensure that all Jews study the Torah and other holy writings in the same fashion and that our prayer books are all alike. With Hebrew as our common religious language, a Jew is able to go into a synagogue in any part of the world and comfortably join in the prayers.

76. Why does the word *chai*, which means "life," also stand for the number eighteen?

In Hebrew, letters are used for reading, writing, and spelling. Each letter also has a numerical value. The word *chai* is spelled with the Hebrew letters *chet* and *yod*. The letter *chet* is eight, and the *yod* is ten. Together, they make eighteen.

Because in Hebrew the word *life* has a numerical value of eighteen, eighteen has become an important number for Jews, often used in jewelry. It is customary to give charity in multiples of eighteen, such as eighteen cents, eighteen dollars, or eighteen hundred dollars. When people give thirty-six dollars, they say that they are giving double *chai,* or eighteen twice.

77. Why is Jerusalem a holy city?

Throughout our history, Jerusalem has been our most central and holy city. It is mentioned in the Bible more than 650 times. Many great religious events have taken place there since the time of Abraham. It was in Jerusalem on Mount Moriah that Abraham almost sacrificed his son, Isaac, but was stopped by the voice of God. King David made Jerusalem the capital and brought the Holy Ark there several times; it was his idea to build the First Temple in Jerusalem. The dream was fulfilled by Solomon, after the death of his father, David.

When the First Temple was destroyed and the Diaspora began, a solemn promise was made by the exiled Jewish people, a promise that has not been forgotten. We find this promise in Psalm 137: "If I forget thee, O Jerusalem, may my right hand lose its cunning, May my tongue cleave to the roof of my mouth, If I remember thee not, If I set not Jerusalem above my chiefest joy."

The Second Temple was also built in Jerusalem, and Jews throughout the ages have traveled great distances to the Holy City to worship. They went there three times a year during the days of the Temple to celebrate the festivals, and they go today to visit the remnant of the Temple—the Western Wall—and to offer prayers in the religious capital.

Several ancient synagogues are located in Jerusalem, as are many ancient Jewish cemeteries, such as the Mount of Olives. Jews also believe that it is from Jerusalem that the Messiah will come.

Other religions, like Roman Catholicism and Islam, also consider Jerusalem to be a holy city. But while Roman Catholics also have Rome and the Vatican, and Muslims have Mecca and Medina, the Jews have only Jerusalem. We face toward Jerusalem during prayer, and we say "Next year in Jerusalem" on Passover and Yom Kippur. During grace after meals we pray for the welfare of Jerusalem. Three times a day, during the recitation of the *Shmoneh Esrei*, we pray for the restoration of Jerusalem. It is our holy and beloved city.

78. Why do we plant trees in Israel?

Planting trees in Israel is one very significant and physical way that those of us in the Diaspora can participate in the development of the land of Israel. Although we're not there ourselves to actually work the land, we can still play a very direct role by sending money to plant trees. In this way we make an important contribution to helping change the landscape, making the land of Israel beautiful, and creating a healthy, productive environment there.

By contributing to the Jewish National Fund, which is responsible for planting millions of trees in Israel, Jews throughout the world have helped make the desert bloom.

Customs and Observances

79. What is the difference between Orthodox, Conservative, Reform, and Reconstructionist Judaism?
Orthodox, Conservative, and Reform are the three main branches of Judaism today; there are many differences between the groups.

Orthodox: Keeps all the traditional laws and customs of the Torah

Conservative: A movement founded in the United States at the end of the nineteenth century that embraces the 613 *mitzvot,* but the interpretation of some laws and customs is more liberal

Reform: A movement founded in Germany that generally emphasizes the spirit of many of the laws and customs but not the laws and customs themselves

Reconstructionist: This youngest branch of American Judaism, born in the twentieth century, is community-oriented with a strong commitment to tradition and to the search for contemporary meaning

80. What does keeping kosher mean?

The Torah has many different dietary laws. It lists those general foods that are permissible, such as fruits and vegetables and most meats, and those that are not permitted, such as shellfish and pork products. There are also certain regulations against cooking or eating meat and dairy products together. Someone who follows all these rules keeps kosher.

A kosher home usually has three sets of dishes, one set for *milchig* (dairy foods), one for *fleishig* (meats), and one for *pareve* (eggs, fish, fruits, vegetables, oils, and grains). There are also three sets of utensils and pots and pans, so that *milchig* foods and *fleishig* foods are never mixed together (*pareve* foods are neutral and may be mixed with either *milchig* or *fleishig*).

In addition, a kosher home will also have three sets of dishes, utensils, and pots and pans set aside for use during Passover (see question 120 regarding keeping kosher for Passover).

There are various local and national agencies that certify that products are kosher, and their certification symbols are printed on the product packaging. The most famous of these agencies is the Union of Orthodox Congregations of America, whose symbol is a capital letter *U* placed inside a circle. Sometimes this symbol is followed by a capital *D*, which means the product contains dairy ingredients. Sometimes the word *pareve* follows the symbol, which means the product can be eaten with either a *milchig* or *fleishig* meal.

There are thousands of products on the market that bear

kosher certification symbols, and each year more and more kosher products are added to grocery store shelves.

The Torah insists that animals be treated kindly. Jews are not allowed to hunt animals for pleasure. Animals used for food must be killed in a special way, which causes them the least amount of suffering possible. The rule against mixing dairy and meat products says, "You shall not seethe a kid in its mother's milk," meaning that it would be the ultimate cruelty to cook an animal in the very liquid (mother's milk) that would nourish it in life.

81. What is a *mezuzah?*

A *mezuzah* is a little parchment scroll on which are written two of the most important passages from the Torah. The scroll is kept inside a decorative case, which is put on the main doorposts of Jewish homes and on the doorposts of other important rooms. As we enter these rooms we kiss the *mezuzah* and we are reminded of the importance of dedicating all our activities to the service of God. This practice is one of the *mitzvot* (commandments) described in many places in the Torah. The passages found in the *mezuzah* are Deuteronomy 6:4–9 and Deuteronomy 11:13–21.

82. What is a *yarmulke,* and why do Jewish men wear one?

A *yarmulke* is a head covering worn to remind us that God is always above our heads. The word *yarmulke* is a combination of two words (*yeru* and *melokha*) and means "fear God." It is sometimes called a *kippah,* or skullcap.

83. What is a *tallit?*

A *tallit* is a four-cornered prayer shawl worn during morning prayers. It is also a special four-cornered garment worn by Orthodox Jews. At each corner of the *tallit* are white and blue fringe, called *tzitzit.* The numerical value of the word *tzitzit* together with the number of knots and threads on the *tzitzit,* equals 613—the number of commandments in the Torah.

A *tallit* is worn because of a commandment in the Bible that requires us to see the fringes, which remind us of the commandments and that we should fulfill them and not turn away from them.

84. What are *tefillin?*

In English, *tefillin* are called phylacteries. They are two small boxes with leather straps attached to them. Inside the boxes are passages from the Bible that relate to the dedication we are supposed to have to God. *Tefillin* are worn by all males over the age of bar mitzvah during morning weekday services.

One box fits squarely between the eyes on the forehead. The other fits on top of the muscle of the forearm. They are worn because of a commandment in the Torah to "put these words on your forearm and on your forehead between your eyes."

We wear them on the forehead to dedicate our thoughts, minds, and creative abilities to God. We wear them on the forearm to remind us to dedicate our strength and physical talents—represented by our muscles—to God. Also, the phylactery on the forearm is supposed to be directly opposite the heart to represent the dedication of our emotions to God.

The other phylactery is worn on the head to represent the dedication of our minds and thinking abilities to God.

85. Why don't traditional women wear *tallit* and *tefillin?*
The Jewish law *Halakah* structures the religious role of Jewish men and women quite differently from the way Western society does. The Torah intends to encourage a value system that promotes and enhances a strong family life, and it recognizes physical and spiritual differences between men and women. Women were considered more spiritual and nurturing than men and, therefore, were believed to have an easier time getting close to God. Because of this more natural relationship with God, women were not required to have as many reminders as men had to keep them on the path of devotion and service to God. Men were given more restrictive religious obligations to keep their attention focused on God despite the distractions they faced out in the world. Women, on the other hand, were freed from certain commandments in the Torah that required a specific action to be done at a specific time, such as wearing a prayer shawl and *tefillin* for morning prayers. In recent years, many non-Orthodox women have chosen to wear *tallit* and *tefillin.*

86. What is a *minyan*, and why is it preferable to pray together with a *minyan?*
Traditionally a *minyan* is a quorum of ten Jewish men older than bar mitzvah age. It is preferable to pray and to do certain other *mitzvot* (like read from the Torah) with a *minyan* because God listens more closely and relates better to a

community of Jews. As a community we strengthen each other, and that communal strength is much greater than all our individual strengths combined together. In recent years, non-Orthodox movements have begun counting women in their *minyan*.

87. What are the most important prayers in Judaism?

There are many prayers for many different occasions, but two standard prayers are said multiple times every day in an observant Jew's life. These are the *Sh'ma* and the *Shmoneh Esrei*, also known as the *Amidah*. *Amidah* means "standing."

The *Sh'ma* is basically three paragraphs that are said by traditional Jews twice a day, morning and evening. It outlines our very basic beliefs in God. The first thing we proclaim in the *Sh'ma* is that we believe that there is a God and that He is one God. We also repeat our commitment to God, and we express our belief in reward and punishment. In addition, we acknowledge that we were put in this world to do good and to keep the *mitzvot*.

The *Sh'ma* is the most fundamental Jewish prayer and has often been said by Jews who realized they were about to die, especially through religious persecution. They said the *Sh'ma* on their deathbeds as a way of affirming their lifelong beliefs and commitment to God.

The other fundamental prayer is *Shmoneh Esrei*, which is at the core of every prayer service. *Shmoneh Esrei* means "eighteen" and is composed of eighteen essential blessings that we request from God. These eighteen things are the important things we need in life, such as health, peace, wisdom, and a sense of justice.

The *Shmoneh Esrei* is the core prayer around which the other prayers in the service are built. If God gave us all the things we requested in the *Shmoneh Esrei*, we would have everything we needed in this life.

88. Why do Jews pray three times a day?

Each of our forefathers is credited with creating one of the three daily prayer services. Abraham initiated the morning prayer; Isaac, the afternoon prayer; and Jacob, the evening prayer. It is meaningful that we begin our day with the devotion of prayer and that we interrupt our daily schedule with prayer during the afternoon service, in that way dedicating our day to God. By ending our day with prayer as well, we look back on the events of the day to see if we can be proud of the way we have conducted ourselves. We think about whether or not our actions were in keeping with the teachings of the Torah and with what God expects from us.

Praying three times a day has been one of the things that has helped to make the Jews an extremely moral people.

89. Are there certain things we pray for and certain things we shouldn't pray for?

Because God feels very close to all humans, we can pray for any real needs that we have. But there are certain things that we should keep in mind when we pray to God.

- We don't always know what is best for ourselves, so

sometimes it is best that we simply ask God to give us what is best for us, whatever that might be.

• We are not supposed to depend on prayer alone. Prayer shows that we have faith in God, but we cannot depend only on prayer. If we are sick, God wants us to do everything in our power to get better, such as go to doctors, take care of ourselves, take necessary medicine, and do whatever we can to improve our health. It is our responsibility to look after ourselves and do whatever we can for ourselves. At the same time we realize that everything ultimately comes from God. The expression "God helps those who help themselves" is in keeping with Jewish tradition.

• Doing good deeds, giving charity, and performing mitzvot, along with saying prayers, are very good and commendable things. But we must never make these mitzvot conditional on our prayers being answered to our satisfaction. In other words, we should never make deals with God. When we pray for someone to recuperate from an illness, it is customary to make a contribution at that time. However, it is improper to make the contribution on the condition that the sick person be healed. That would be like testing God. The contribution should be made in the merit of the sick person, and it is hoped that the combination of the good deed and the prayer will give the sick person a reprieve from his or her illness.

• We should never pray for frivolous things, like our favorite baseball team winning the pennant.

90. Why don't we kneel when we pray?
The only place where Jews knelt during prayer was in the

Holy Temple in Jerusalem. Prostrating oneself is considered the ultimate sign of submission and devotion to the Creator. It is certainly something that should not be done on a regular or habitual basis. Only in the Temple, where God's presence reigned with great intensity, did Jews exhibit such extraordinarily high levels of devotion. The only exception to this rule takes place sometimes on the most solemn days of the year during the Rosh Hashana and Yom Kippur services. It is the practice in some synagogues to kneel during the portion of the service that evokes the memories of the great and Holy Temple in Jerusalem.

91. Is there a book of Jewish prayers?
Yes, in fact there are two books of Jewish prayers. One is used for weekdays and the Sabbath (Shabbat), and one is used for the High Holy Days. The Shabbat and weekday prayer book is called the *siddur. Siddur* is taken from the Hebrew word *seder,* which means "order"—the order of our prayers. The holiday prayer book is called a *machzor,* which stands for the "cycle" of our prayers.

92. Why is it important to go to services?
Although God listens to all of our prayers, wherever and whenever we pray, it is more likely that our prayers will be answered when we pray with a *minyan.* God joins all of our good qualities together and looks at us as a group with many worthy characteristics, rather than as individuals with a number of flaws and shortcomings.

Also, when we attend services or become members of a synagogue, we're becoming more active Jews and are more likely to participate in activities concerning the Jewish community. Whenever our people get together, we tend to get involved in worthy projects. These projects can include charities, art and music appreciation, and community service. Attending services generally leads to getting involved in these types of positive activities.

Perhaps the most important reason for going to services is that it makes us feel closer to God. When we worship Him in the synagogue with the beautiful Torah scrolls present, the cantor's lovely chanting, and the words of the rabbi to guide us, we leave the synagogue feeling uplifted and with a stronger sense of our Jewish selves.

93. Why do some Jews wear black coats, hats, and beards?

In addition to taking on cultural traditions of the many countries from which Jews have come, we have also developed different religious traditions and customs. That's why you'll see many religious Jews, such as Hasidim, dressed in different fashions or having different customs. They are dressing in the manner of their ancestors, who came from communities in Europe where such dress was common. Even styles of hats and earlocks that Jews wear will differ, depending on the European community of their ancestors.

94. What are Hasidim?

Hasidim, or Hasidic Jews, follow a form of Orthodox Judaism that was developed first by the Baal Shem Tov, a *rebbe* (teacher) who lived in the early 1700s. He called on his students to follow a more emotional, intense form of Judaism, which involved a lot more praying and singing and sense of spirit than had been practiced before. His students formed Hasidic communities throughout Europe, and these communities have continued strongly up to the present time, remaining true to the teaching of the Baal Shem Tov and his students.

About twenty-five Hasidic communities are still in existence today. The one most people are familiar with is the Lubavitch movement. People in Hasidic communities still hold to the traditional dress of their European ancestors and live in close-knit groups in large cities throughout the world.

95. What is a *minhag*?

A *minhag* is a tradition, or custom (as opposed to a law), practiced in one geographic location or in one community. This local custom might not be practiced in another community and may even be the complete opposite of a tradition practiced somewhere else.

While these traditions don't have the full impact of the law, they have become part of the way things are done in a community and are considered sacred in their own right and are not to be broken.

An example of how a *minhag* works in two different communities can be found in the use of corn during Passover—whether it is to be considered *hametz* or not. In Mediterranean communities, like Spain, Morocco, Lebanon, Syria, and other Sephardic communities, corn has always been permitted during Passover. In European, or Ashkenazic, communities corn has not been permitted since the Middle Ages.

The Torah specifically prohibits the use of leavened flours (flour made from grains, such as oats, barley, and wheat) during Passover. During the Middle Ages in European communities the distinction between corn flour and these other types of flour became blurred. The flours were often stored together and mixed together. Because of this, the rabbis eventually decided to prohibit the use of all flours, including corn and bean flour, during Passover. In this way, it became the European tradition, or *minhag*, to prohibit any products made of corn and beans.

In the Mediterranean communities there was never any problem distinguishing corn flour from others, so it became the tradition to prohibit only those flours mentioned in the Torah.

Even today, we might find two families living next door to each other—the one of Sephardic descent using corn and bean products during Passover and the one of Ashkenazic descent not doing so, each following their own custom, or *minhag*. Each family will be equally religious and acceptable in practicing their tradition. Jewish law teaches us that we are to respect our family traditions almost as if they were law. We must honor and keep our traditions and respect each other's traditions. The Torah uses the phrase "these and these [meaning both these customs] are God's living Torah," and we must respect them.

There are many other customs, some of which involve the order in which prayers are said during services, some of which involve naming traditions, and other matters that vary from country to country. The fundamentals of the Torah never change, but some of the traditions that add a little something special to our practices are different.

96. What is *tzedakah*?

The word *tzedakah* means "righteousness," which we interpret to mean "charity." There are many forms of charity found in the Torah, for example, tithing, which means giving a tenth of your income to charity. In the times of the Temple there was the practice of giving a specific coin—the half shekel—toward the construction of the Temple. There were special gifts that people gave to help the operation of the Temple and other gifts that were to be used as offerings during services in the Temple. There are specific commandments on how we are supposed to help our poorer brethren.

So charity is ingrained within the personality of the Jew throughout the pages of the Torah and Talmud. A great portion of our studies deals with how to give charity, when to give charity, and what to give as charity. The reason charity is so central to being a Jew is that it is one of the key elements of our Jewish identity.

We give charity to further recognize the good that God has given us. God has made our lives full and good, even if we don't have much money, possessions, or impressive achievements. There is still so much for which to be thankful to God, for He has given us many gifts: the gift of life, the gift of health, and the gift of love. When we give charity, we're extending that same kindness that God has given to us. We're passing it on to the next person, who passes it on to the next, filling up the whole world with this good-ness.

That is why the Talmud says that the world stands on three things: the study of Torah, because without the study of Torah we wouldn't know what to do; *avodah,* which means the service of God, because we have to recognize that there is a God and that we have to serve Him before we can understand the third thing, which is *gemilut hasedem,* acts of kindness performed in recognition that all good comes from God. He starts the process, and then we spread it around until the whole world is enveloped in a circle of goodness.

97. What is a *pushke?*

A *pushke* is a traditional coin box that used to be part of every Jewish home. It was customary for each member of the family to drop coins into the *pushke* before the start of Shabbat and holidays as a means of giving to charity.

One of the most famous kinds of *pushkes,* or *tzedakah* boxes, is the Jewish National Fund Blue Box, which played a large role in the establishment of the State of Israel. In Eastern European homes, families would deposit money in a box in order to purchase the land that became the State of Israel. There are *tzedakah* boxes for many different chari-ties, and the way they work is quite simple. Small amounts of money are collected from each family, but together, when many, many families contribute, the total becomes quite large. When everyone gives *tzedakah,* we work to-gether and are able to do great things as a community.

The Jewish Calendar and Its Holidays

98. What are the months of the Hebrew calendar?

The names of the Hebrew months are *Nisan, Iyar, Sivan, Tammuz, Av, Elul, Tishrei, Cheshvan, Kislev, Tevet, Shevat,* and *Adar.* (During a leap year, there is *Adar I* and *Adar II.*)

99. Why doesn't Rosh Hashana or the other Jewish holidays come out on the same secular date each year?

The Jewish calendar is very different from the secular, or Gregorian, calendar. The Jewish calendar is a lunar calendar, which means it is based on the moon. Each month begins with the appearance of the new moon and ends with the appearance of the next moon.

The secular calendar is a solar calendar, meaning that it is based on the earth's revolution around the sun. The secular calendar has, of course, 365 days in it, with one day added every four years as a leap day. The Jewish calendar has approximately 354 days in it. So the Jewish holidays don't come out exactly on the same secular date each year, because there is an eleven-day difference in our annual calendars.

100. If there is an eleven-day difference in our calendars, why isn't there a greater difference between the two calendars? Wouldn't a holiday like Rosh Hashana come out in December or January after a few years?

No. The Jewish calendar has an elaborate leap-year system. The great sage Hillel set up our calendar for permanent record about two thousand years ago. Using Hillel's system, seven out of every nineteen years has an added month to it. The month that is added is called *Adar Bet*, or *Adar II*.

A Jewish leap year has thirteen months. It doesn't have just an added day, it has an added month. Through this system our holidays stay in season. Rosh Hashana always comes out in the fall, Hanukkah in the winter, and Passover in the spring.

101. Why do Jewish days start at sundown?

This is another big difference between the Jewish and secular calendars. The Jewish day begins in the evening because God created the darkness first and then the light. It says in the Bible: "And there was evening, and there was morning, one day." This is why Shabbat and all holidays begin at sundown. For example, Shabbat begins on Friday night, Yom Kippur begins on Kol Nidre evening, and the Seder takes place on the evening before the first day of Passover.

Personal observances also begin in the evening. For instance, a *yahrzeit* candle is lit on the evening before the anniversary of a loved one's death.

102. Why do Jewish calendars list the year 2000 as 5760?
The Jewish calendar records time beginning with the creation of the world as told by the Bible. According to tradition, that took place 5,760 years ago (from 2000). The secular calendar uses the birth of Christ as its starting point.

103. Why is the Jewish New Year in the fall instead of on January first?
The Jewish holiday Rosh Hashana is our New Year. It is the anniversary of the day that God created Adam, the first human.

The Jewish calendar has twelve months, just like the secular calendar. The first month is *Tishrei*. On the first day of *Tishrei* each year is Rosh Hashana—the new year.

104. Why are Rosh Hashana and Yom Kippur called the High Holidays?
This period of time, the first ten days of the year, has many names and titles. Rosh Hashana means "the head of the year" and is our New Year's Day. It is also called the Day of Judgment. Rosh Hashana is also the first day of the Ten Days of Repentance ending on Yom Kippur (which means "Day of Atonement," or forgiveness). Another name for these days is the Days of Awe. What all these names and titles indicate is that these ten days are very special days in the Jewish calendar.

Unlike the secular New Year, which is a time for parties, the Jewish New Year is a serious time. Jewish heritage teaches us that at the beginning of each year God takes a very close look at the whole world and all the individuals in it and makes a judgment. Those that have been clearly very good during the past year are immediately judged on Rosh Hashana as being worthy of reward and good things. Those that have been exceptionally bad are judged for an evil decree. But most people are somewhere in between and have to make some adjustments.

During this solemn time of year we are given the opportunity to reflect on our ways and our previous behavior and to see if there are improvements that we can make in our lives. This process of taking a look at our past behavior, thinking about it very carefully, feeling regret for our sins, and then deciding to improve and to commit ourselves to that goal, is called *teshuvah,* or "repentance." In these ten days at the beginning of the year, God gives us humans a tremendous opportunity. We are able to reflect on our sins and clean our slates. When we take this process seriously and want to improve, God gives us total forgiveness. A person can do *teshuvah* at any time, but God created a special time of the year when He is especially sympathetic and forgiving. This time has come to be known as the High Holidays because through these days of prayer and thoughtfulness an individual can reach very high and lofty spiritual levels and attain a closeness to God.

105. What is a shofar and why do we blow it on Rosh Hashana?

Sounding the shofar (ram's horn) on Rosh Hashana is a biblical commandment, and it is done for many reasons. First, the shofar is like the clarion call, or trumpet, that was sounded before kings of old. The shofar sound on Rosh Hashana reminds us that God is our king who created humankind on this very day and that we are His servants who obey His commandments.

The shofar sound is also a call to wake us out of our complacency (feelings of satisfaction with ourselves) and to encourage us to think of the importance and awesomeness of Rosh Hashana and the need for *teshuvah* (repentance).

The shofar also reminds us of important events in Jewish history. When the Jews received the Torah they heard the piercing sound of the shofar at Mount Sinai, marking that great event. On Rosh Hashana we are reminded of all the responsibilities and commandments of the Torah given to us that day at Mount Sinai and that we should think about whether we have kept the commandments properly and honored our responsibilities.

Also, the sounding of the ram's horn reminds us of the story of the binding of Isaac, our forefather, by Abraham, which is told in the first book of the Bible. Abraham was willing to sacrifice his beloved son, Isaac, in honor of God. God showed Abraham that He did not want him to actually sacrifice his son. Instead Abraham sacrificed a ram. We remind ourselves of the ultimate loyalty we owe to God, a loyalty demonstrated by Isaac and Abraham. We are inspired by their devotion, and we ask God to remember the faithfulness of our great ancestors. We ask God to be lenient and merciful with us because of their goodness.

The blast of the shofar also sounds like sobbing. We ask God in His mercy to remember not only our own tears while we cry for forgiveness but also the tears of all Jews, past and present, who have suffered because they were Jewish. We ask God to please deal with us kindly. With humble tears, we look to the Almighty to remember the Jews of Israel and other lands who cry out to be free from terrorism and to remember the tears of the millions of Jews who died during the Holocaust and the many other torturous times in our history. We hope that in their honor the New Year that is coming will be a year of peace and freedom for all people.

106. What does the blessing *L'shana tova tikatevu* mean?

L'shana tova tikatevu is a traditional blessing that Jews around the world use to wish each other well during the High Holidays. It means "May you be written for a good year." The Talmud tells us that during this period of judgment God conducts a heavenly courtroom and judges every individual. On Rosh Hashana He writes each person's name in one of two books, the Book of Life or the Book of Punishment. The decree is written down on Rosh Hashana but it is not until Yom Kippur that the decree is sealed. Between Rosh Hashana and Yom Kippur the decision could be changed based on a person's behavior and level of repentance. That is why we greet each other with this blessing.

During this time of year it is customary to do many extra *mitzvot,* like doing extra charity, visiting the sick, going to synagogue more often, all in the hope that we will gain additional merits to our account.

107. What is *tashlich?*

Tashlich means "to cast." It comes from the phrase in the prayer book in which we ask God "to cast our sins to the depths of the sea." A very beautiful custom has developed around this prayer. During the Ten Days of Repentance it has become a tradition to go to a stream, river, or brook and say certain prayers beseeching God to bury our sins and transgressions out of sight in the depths of the water. We empty our pockets of small crumbs, which are swallowed by the fish in the water. This is a symbol of the cleansing and vanquishing of our sins.

108. Why do we eat apples and honey on Rosh Hashana?

There are many customs that Jews around the world practice on Rosh Hashana that involve symbolic foods. Eating these sweet foods demonstrates our desire that God will bless us with a sweet year. Eating apples and honey is the most famous custom. Another custom is to eat pomegranates to symbolize that our lives should be full of *mitzvot* and other good things, just as a pomegranate is so full of sweet seeds.

109. Why do we fast on Yom Kippur?

Yom Kippur is the most solemn and serious day of the year. We spend the whole day in the synagogue praying for our own welfare and for the welfare of Jews around the world. It is the last of the Ten Days of Awe, Repentance, and Judgment. It is fitting that adults or those who are over bar or bat mitzvah age don't eat anything all day. Judaism doesn't teach self-deprivation (denying ourselves those things we need to maintain a healthy, comfortable life), and we are not supposed to inflict pain on ourselves needlessly. But on this holiest day, when we are being judged, we wish to deprive ourselves of our usual pleasures to show God our devotion and dedication to spirituality. We don't want to busy ourselves with our physical desires, such as eating, on this day.

It is interesting to note that the Talmud says that in preparation for the Day of Judgment and fasting, it is a great *mitzvah* to eat the day before Yom Kippur, so that we are properly prepared for Yom Kippur. For that reason, we always eat an especially large meal on *Erev* Yom Kippur, before *Kol Nidre*.

110. What is *Kol Nidre?*

Kol Nidre is the prayer that begins the Yom Kippur service on the eve of Yom Kippur. It asks for forgiveness in case we have made any promises or vows during the past year that we haven't kept. Honesty is one of the most important virtues expected of us by God. If we are not honest, we must seek forgiveness from God prior to the start of Yom Kippur. Before we can ask for forgiveness from God on Yom Kippur we must think through our past actions to see if there was anyone with whom we weren't fair or honest or if there was anyone we had argued with during the past year; if so, we must make amends with this person. It can't be expected that God will be forgiving of us if we are not forgiving of each other.

111. Why do we light candles on Hanukkah?

About two thousand years ago, during the time of the Jews'

Second Temple in Israel, the Greeks and their powerful empire tried to do away with the Jewish religion and even successfully conquered the Jews' Holy Temple.

There was a great warrior named Mattathias, the head of the Hasmonean family, who against all odds led the Jews to a great victory over the Greeks and reconquered the Temple. One of Mattathias' five sons, the most brilliant warrior of all, was the legendary Judah Maccabeus. According to the legend, when the Jewish soldiers entered the Temple after the battle, they were saddened to discover that the entire Temple was overturned and defiled. To their great dismay, there was only one flask of pure olive oil left. The pure olive oil was important because exactly one flask was needed to light the menorah each day as part of the religious ceremony in the Temple service.

To the Jews' great wonderment and surprise, a miracle happened and the oil lasted for eight full days, until they could complete the process of pressing new pure olive oil.

To commemorate this miracle of the oil and our great victory over the Greeks, who tried to destroy our religion, we celebrate Hanukkah for eight days, and each night we light a special menorah called a *hanukkiyah*.

112. What does Hanukkah mean?

There are two meanings. The literal translation of *Hanukkah* is "dedication," referring to the rededication of the Temple after reclaiming it from the Greeks. The second meaning is acronymic (an acronym is a word formed by combining the first parts or letters of several words). In Hebrew, *hanu*, which means "we rested," and the letters that numerically equal the number twenty-five, combine to spell out the word *Hanukkah*. The number twenty-five refers to the twenty-fifth day of the Hebrew month *Kislev*, which is the Hebrew date on which we celebrate Hanukkah each year.

113. Where did the game of dreidel come from?

During Hanukkah, children all over the world play the traditional game of dreidel. A dreidel is a kind of four-sided spinning top. One each of the four sides are printed one of the following four Hebrew letters: *nun, gimel, hay,* and *shin.* The four letters stand for the Hebrew words: *Nes gadol hayah sham,* which means "a great miracle happened there."

The story of how dreidel playing became a Jewish tradition is fascinating. While the Greeks were trying to destroy the Jewish religion, they banned the study of Torah in public. To get around the ban, Jewish children would get together with their teachers and study Torah in secret places. If they heard Greek soldiers or informers approaching, they would quickly hide their books, take out a top, and begin playing. The Greeks would be fooled. When the Greeks left, the children and their teachers would go back to studying the Torah.

So on Hanukkah we play dreidel to remind ourselves of the victory, the heroism of the Jewish children at that time, and our good fortune that we can study Torah openly in the society that we live in today.

It is interesting that dreidels made in Israel have different letters on them. They read: *nun, gimel, shin, pay,* which stand for: *Nes gadol hayah po,* which means "a great miracle happened *here,*" because the victory of Hanukkah happened in Israel.

114. Why do we eat latkes on Hanukkah?

Latkes are potato pancakes fried in oil. It has become customary to eat delicious foods fried in oil on Hanukkah to remind us of the miracle of the oil. In Israel, doughnuts are a popular treat for the same reason. All Jewish holidays have their own special treats. Most are in one way or another a symbol of that holiday's particular celebration.

115. Is Hanukkah like the Jewish Christmas?

No. There is no relationship between the two holidays. It just so happens that they often fall at the same time of year, and so Jews and Gentiles tend to wish each other "Happy Holidays." But there is no religious connection between the two.

116. Why is Pesach called Passover, and why do we eat matzo on this holiday?

Pesach (or Passover) is an eight-day holiday that takes place in the spring. It celebrates the Jews being freed from slavery three thousand years ago.

At that time all the people of Israel lived in Egypt. For about two hundred years their freedom was taken away from them and our ancestors actually became lowly slaves to the evil Egyptian kings, called pharoahs. During most of those two hundred years, our people did not even have real bread to eat. They had to subsist on hard "slave bread" called matzo. It didn't have any yeast or eggs in it like regular bread, only flour and water.

Moses became our leader during those days, and he was instructed by God to take the Jews out of Egypt. But the pharoah would not listen to Moses and refused to let the Jews leave the land of Egypt and go up to their native country of Israel. God had to inflict many punishments on the Egyptians before the pharoah finally gave up and allowed the Jews to leave Egypt. These punishments are called "the Ten Plagues."

The night the Jews finally left Egypt against the pharoah's will, the last and harshest of the Ten Plagues was brought on the Egyptian people. All the firstborn Egyptian children were killed. The Bible tells how the Angel of Death visited every Egyptian home and smote their firstborn. But he did not visit any of the Jewish homes. The Bible relates how the homes of the Jews were "passed over" (*pesach*, in Hebrew), and that's why we call this holiday Passover.

That night the Jews left so hurriedly that they still didn't get a chance to bake real bread for their trip. They only had time to bake their regular slave bread, the matzo. To remember the days of slavery and our miraculous escape, we eat matzo during Pesach.

117. What is the Seder?

The Seder is the large festive family meal that we have on the first two nights of Passover. At this meal we retell the stories of the terrible things that happened to the Jewish people while they were enslaved in Egypt and recount all the exciting miracles that happened when they were re-deemed from slavery. The Seder is one of the richest traditions of the Jewish people.

The episode in our history when God took us out of Egypt marks what is probably the most important event of our people's past. The redemption from slavery in Egypt was a turning point. At that point our forefathers became a nation and our relationship with God was solidified.

The Talmud says that every Jew should consider it as if he himself was redeemed from slavery.

118. Why do we ask the four questions?

The Torah instructs every parent to explain all the stories about Pesach to their children. That is why part of the Seder is done in a question-and-answer format, so that the children can ask, and the parents can answer. The Seder and our tradition of telling and retelling the beautiful story of Passover is one of our people's greatest and most unique traditions. For thousands of years parents have handed down the great epic of freedom from generation to generation. Wherever Jews have been, in good times and bad, we have never deprived ourselves of this beautiful custom.

There are many, many stories of how Jews went to great lengths to continue the practice of conducting a Seder. In concentration camps and in the Warsaw ghetto during World War II, people sacrificed their lives to have a Seder with their families. During the Spanish Inquisition of the thirteenth and fourteenth centuries, families pretended to accept the Christian faith to save their lives, but when Passover came around, they conducted the Seder in secret tunnels underneath their homes and thus kept our traditions alive.

The Seder is a good example of how Judaism places great emphasis on transmitting our heritage from one generation to another.

119. What is the *Haggadah?*

The *Haggadah* is the special book we use to guide us through the Seder. It contains all the various prayers we say, songs we sing, and customs we practice on the Seder night. There are many *Haggadah* manuscripts in museums throughout the world. Many beautiful editions are hundreds and even thousands of years old. There are artistic renditions of the *Haggadah* from every era and every land that Jews have lived in. There are also many different modern *Haggadot* with English translations, instructions, and commentaries, so that even people who do not read or understand Hebrew can conduct a Seder with all of its rich traditions.

120. What does kosher for Passover mean?

As part of the commemoration of Passover, we do not eat bread for the whole eight days of Pesach, remembering the matzo that our ancestors ate in Egypt. The Torah prohibits us from eating any leavened flour during Pesach. Flour that is leavened contains yeast or other ingredients, like eggs, that cause it to rise. Leavened flour is called *hametz* in Hebrew. Any food product that has *hametz* in it cannot be eaten on Pesach—not only bread but things like cakes and cookies as well. That's why during Passover, traditional Jews eat only foods that are kosher for Passover, which means that the food has been inspected by a rabbi to be sure that no *hametz* ingredients or processes were used in preparing it.

121. Why do a lot of people make a big deal out of cleaning their house for Passover?

The Torah says that *hametz* should not be found anywhere in your household or possession during Passover. Traditional Jews clean their entire home to make sure there are no cake or bread crumbs anywhere in the house before the start of Passover.

122. What is *Yom Hashoah?*

Yom Hashoah is the day marking the memory of all the people lost in the Holocaust. We pause for a moment on that day to remember the innocent men, women, and children who died during the Nazi era. Throughout the world, special commemorative services are held in their honor.

123. What is *Yom Hazikaron?*

Yom Hazikaron is the Israeli Memorial Day on which Jews remember all the fallen Israeli soldiers who died in defense of the State of Israel. We remember the soldiers, many of them young boys and girls, who bravely gave their lives to help create and protect the State of Israel.

In the State of Israel, sirens wail at 11 A.M. at the start of memorial services in the military cemeteries. It is a quiet and somber day and places of entertainment are closed. At 7 P.M., a special memorial ceremony takes place at Mount Herzl. Following the service, sirens blast once more, marking the end of *Yom Hazikaron* and the beginning of Israel's Independence Day, *Yom Ha Atzma'ut*.

124. What is *Yom Ha Atzma'ut?*

Yom Ha Atzma'ut is the day on which we celebrate the creation of the State of Israel. This occurred in 1948. Following the end of *Yom Hazikaron*, Israelis dance and sing, celebrating late into the night and on into the early hours of the next day. Some Israelis dance and sing in the streets, while others gather in their homes to celebrate. Most Israelis spend the following day on picnics and other outings.

125. What is *Yom Yerushalayim?*

Yom Yerushalayim, or Jerusalem Day, celebrates the anniversary of the 1967 reunification of the city of Jerusalem. On that day during the Six-Day War, Israeli soldiers reclaimed the area of Jerusalem that had been under Jordanian control. For the first time since the Jordanian occupation of 1948, Jews had access to all of Jerusalem and were again able to pray at their holiest shrine, the Western Wall.

126. Why do some Jews celebrate holidays for two days and some celebrate them for only one?

In the days before Hillel first worked out the fixed calendar of the Jewish months and holidays, the start of the new month was determined by the *Sanhedrin*. They based this on the testimony of two witnesses who claimed they had seen the new moon. Once the *Sanhedrin* determined that a new month had in fact begun, bonfires were lit from mountaintop to mountaintop as a signal, so that everyone would know when to begin the month. In this way, they would also know when to celebrate any holidays that fell during that month.

In later times, messengers were sent to the Jews in the Diaspora to tell them that the new month had begun. Because the messengers often had to travel great distances, it became the custom in the Diaspora to add an extra day to certain holidays just to be sure the holiday was celebrated at the proper time. These holidays are Pesach, Shavuot, and Sukkot.

Even after Hillel created the permanent calendar and Jews everywhere knew for a fact when the holidays were, it remained the custom to celebrate these holidays for an extra day in the Diaspora to remember that our ancestors had always done so.

These holidays have always been celebrated for only one day in Israel, because of the close proximity to the *Sanhedrin* in ancient days. In fact, an Israeli who happens to be visiting outside of Israel during one of these holidays will follow the Israeli custom and observe only one day. Reform Jews have shortened the observance of some holidays to one day.

127. Why is there so much partying on Purim?

Purim is a Jewish holiday that takes place each year one month before Passover. About twenty-three hundred years ago a very evil diplomat named Haman lived in Persia (today's Iran). He was one of the highest advisers to the powerful Ahasuerus, king of Persia. Haman came from the dynasty of Amalek, the forsworn and mortal enemies of the

Jews from the time we were wandering in the desert on the way to the Promised Land of Israel. The Amalekites were always at the forefront of attacks on Jews. Even in modern times, whenever notorious and pathological enemies like Hitler and the Nazis rise up against us, we see them as the descendants of the tribe of Amalek. Although we are a peace-loving people the Torah commands us never to forget the evilness of the Amalekites and what they did to us when we were wandering in the desert. Making noise on Purim serves to blot out their names and thereby dishonor their memory.

Haman was always plotting against the Jews. One time it seemed that he would succeed. He convinced Ahasuerus to put a bounty on every Jew's head, and he promised to pay huge sums of money to the treasury and to add all the Jews' wealth to the treasury as well. He convinced Ahasuerus to encourage all the people of Persia to kill every Jew in the land. (This shows us that Hitler was not the first evil leader to try to blame an entire country's problems on the Jews and to seek a "final solution" to these problems by killing all the Jews. In every generation there have been enemies eager to wipe out the Jews. Haman and Hitler are only two of many such villains.)

Through a series of seeming coincidences, a great heroine named Esther, who was secretly a Jew, was Ahasuerus' queen at that time. Under the guidance of her uncle Mordecai, who was one of the Jewish sages, she had never revealed to King Ahasuerus that she was Jewish. When things looked as if they couldn't get worse, Mordecai told her to go to the king and reveal her true identity. She convinced the king that killing the Jews would be very bad for his empire and that Haman was an evil tyrant. Ahasuerus was so enraged with Haman that he had him and his whole family killed. He issued a decree that allowed the Jews to mobilize and defend themselves. They were very successful, and the Jews avoided a great calamity.

We celebrate this amazing turnaround with the holiday of Purim, which is the happiest and most joyous festival in the Jewish calendar.

128. What is the *Megillah?*

The *Megillah* is a scroll that tells all the fascinating details of the Purim story. Each year Jews gather in the synagogue on Purim and listen to the telling of the story in Hebrew. This is called the *Megillah* reading.

129. Why do we use noisemakers on Purim?

As part of the excitement of the celebration, whenever the name of the evil Haman is mentioned in the *Megillah,* we make a lot of noise—as if to wipe out any remembrance or mention of him. The Torah says that we should erase the memory of Amalek—Haman's ancestry. In the olden days people would take two blocks of wood and write the word *Amalek* on one of them. When Haman's name was mentioned they would knock the blocks together until the word would be scraped off. Would that make a racket! Some people would write the name Amalek on the soles of their shoes and stamp their feet—that would make a lot of noise too. Today in Israel and around the world, some synagogues allow the use of modern noisemakers—car horns, stereo speakers, boom boxes, you name it—all in the same noisy tradition of wiping out the memory of Amalek.

130. What is *Shalach Monos?*

Shalach Monos, sometimes called *mishloach manot,* means "sending presents." Some of the most important *mitzvot* on Purim are sending gifts of food to our friends and giving *tzedakah*—charity—to the poor. This is to highlight one of the important aspects of the story of Purim: Jewish unity. There were thousands of Jews in Persia, but not one gave away the secret that Queen Esther was Jewish. If Haman had known that, he could have plotted to kill her first so that he could get away with his bigger plot—to kill all the Jews. But because the Jews were unified, he never found out, and Esther was able to intervene and save her people.

There were also other examples of Jewish unity throughout the Purim story, such as Jews banding together to fight off their enemies. So one of the things we celebrate is our unity and love for one another. That is why we have the custom of sending gifts to one another. We also give money to the poor because we don't want to leave any Jewish person out of the celebration, and we want to make sure that on this day even the poorest among us are having a very happy day.

131. What are some of the other festive rituals that take place on Purim?

Another *mitzvah* on Purim is to have a great feast to celebrate our victory. At this feast we usually eat three-cornered pastries called hamantaschen, which remind us of Haman's three-cornered hat.

Purim is also the one day each year when drinking to make us happy is part of the celebration. While we enjoy drinking wine on Shabbat and other holidays, we do so in moderation. But Purim is the only day on which Jews are encouraged to drink beyond moderation. Of course the Torah does not allow us to endanger our health, so even on this day, while drinking is permitted, it is permitted only for adults—who must drink in a responsible manner.

Another popular form of celebration is the Purim *spiel*. *Spiel* means "play." On Purim we put on humorous plays about the *Megillah* and other stories. This is also a time for putting on masquerades, wearing disguises, and generally having a fun time.

It is a day of great joy and hope, because we are reminded that even in the midst of a terrible plot, things can always turn around for the good.

132. What is Lag Ba'Omer?

Lag Ba'Omer is a holiday that began in the days of Rabbi Akiva, a great Talmudic scholar. A terrible plague claimed the lives of Rabbi Akiva's twenty-four thousand students. This happened to occur during the *omer*, which is the period of time between Passover and Shavuot. Each year Jews have always counted the forty-nine days between these two holidays, one of which signifies our freedom from slavery and the other which celebrates the giving of the Torah. On the thirty-third day of the *omer*, miraculously, none of the students died. (The word *lag* is equal to the number thirty-three in Hebrew.)

The holiday is usually celebrated with picnics and other outdoor activities, including celebrating around bonfires. There is no school in Israel on Lag Ba'Omer so that children can spend the day playing and celebrating outdoors.

133. What is Tu B'Shevat?

Tu B'Shevat is the holiday celebrating the birthday of all trees. It takes place on the fifteenth day of *Shevat*. We celebrate by eating various fruits and nuts, especially those grown in Israel. In Israel, people plant new trees on Tu B'Shevat, which has become an Israeli Arbor Day. Schoolchildren make field trips to plant new trees and enjoy a day of nature.

134. Why is Tisha B'Av such a sad holiday?

Tisha B'Av (the ninth day of *Av*) is the day that marks the destruction of both Temples. It is also the day on which Moses broke the first tablets containing the Ten Commandments because he came down from Mount Sinai to find that the Jews had turned away from God. During the three-week period between the seventeenth of *Tammuz* and the ninth of *Av*, many other tragic events in Jewish history took place. So Tisha B'Av brings to a close this three-week period of mourning for sorrowful events in our Jewish past.

135. What is the holiday of Sukkot?

The holiday of Sukkot is a harvest festival and begins four days after Yom Kippur. It lasts for seven days and is followed by the Simchat Torah holiday. The word *sukkot* is plural for *sukkah*, which means "booth." The holiday takes its name from the booths, or sheds, or temporary houses that we erect as part of the celebration.

136. How is a *sukkah* made?

A *sukkah* is created as a temporary structure, not a permanent one. The walls can be made of any material, but the ceilings must be made out of greenery or anything that grows from the ground, such as bamboo poles or evergreen branches. The ceiling cannot be permanently constructed and must be at least partially open to the sky so that we can see the stars.

These booths can be any size as long as they are larger than about three feet by three feet. The greenery covering the *sukkah* is called *schach*.

137. What do we do with a *sukkah* on Sukkot and why?

The Torah tells us that during the forty years that the Jews were wandering in the desert before they came to the Promised Land of Israel, they lived in tents or temporary homes. Sometimes while they were traveling they didn't even have tents—it was only God's protection that they could depend on.

The Torah teaches us that God provided special clouds to protect His people from the harsh environment of the desert. These clouds traveled before the Jews, behind them, and above them and are called "the Clouds of Glory."

So on the holiday of Sukkot we temporarily go out of our homes and "dwell" in booths to remember how God took us out of Egypt and provided shelter for us in the desert on the way to Israel.

138. But what does all this have to do with us today?

Quite a lot. Nowadays most of us live in fairly comfortable homes with the modern conveniences of heating and air-conditioning, indoor plumbing, electrical conveniences, and so on. We tend to take our homes and their comforts for granted. It is very easy to forget about the One we must have faith in and give thanks to for the good things in our life.

Our homes seem so permanent and secure that once a year we go into very humble and insecure "shanties" and we remember that everything, even our big and comfortable houses, really comes from God. We cover the roof of the *sukkah* with greenery to remind us that it is fall—harvest time—and ultimately everything, the harvest, crops, weather, and land, comes from God and His good graces. He controls the natural forces in the world, and everything that we have, including our secure homes, which protect us from the elements, comes from His bounty.

139. What do we do in the *sukkah*?

The Torah tells us that for seven days we should make ourselves comfortable in a *sukkah* as if it were our home. Therefore, it has become customary to decorate our *sukkot* very attractively and to eat our meals in them—weather permitting, of course. There are many people who sleep in their *sukkah* each night during the holiday. There are also many neighborhoods in Israel where *sukkot* are built onto the homes as patios. Of course, the top has to be temporary, so they have devised electronic roofs that roll away at the push of a button and are replaced by *schach* (greenery) for the Sukkot holiday.

140. What is a *lulav* and *etrog*?

A *lulav* is a palm branch and an *etrog* is a citrus fruit, called a citron, which looks much like a lemon. The *lulav* and *etrog* are part of "the four kinds" (of plants) that were held together during the Sukkot services in the Temple in Jerusalem. The other two kinds of plants are a myrtle branch and a willow branch.

At this time, when we give thanks to God for an abundant harvest, these four agricultural items are used to represent the huge variety of agricultural products with which God blesses the earth. In modern times we wave these four items together in the synagogue during the Sukkot festival.

141. What is Shmini Atzeret?

Shmini Atzeret is a holiday that falls on the eighth day of Sukkot, following a long string of Jewish holidays that begins with Rosh Hashana. Whereas the other holidays celebrate specific events, Shmini Atzeret is a day when God in effect says to the Jewish people, "Stay with Me just one day more so that we can enjoy being together just for the sake of being together."

It is similar to what often happens when a family celebrates a wedding and relatives come from out of town to share in the festivities. Following the wedding and all the parties connected with it, the relatives will often gather together "one more time" just to enjoy each other's company before returning to their regular schedules.

Shmini Atzeret is a day set aside for us to spend a little more time with God after the holidays are over and before celebrating the final autumn holiday, Simchat Torah.

142. What is Simchat Torah?

Simchat Torah is the holiday that immediately follows Sukkot. It falls on the eighth day of Sukkot and celebrates the conclusion of one complete cycle of the reading of the Torah. It is combined with Shmini Atzeret in Israel but celebrated as a ninth day of Sukkot in the Diaspora. This holiday reflects our tremendous joy in having read the entire Torah and our excitement and anticipation as we immediately begin the cycle of Torah reading once again.

Because the Torah is the most important aspect of a Jew's life, Simchat Torah is almost like a birthday celebration. We celebrate our having reached this time and that we have the opportunity to begin reading the Torah again. It is a joyous holiday, special not only for adults but for children, who are encouraged to share in the delight of learning Torah.

143. Why do we celebrate Shabbat?

Shabbat, or the Sabbath, is a weekly celebration of God's creation of the world. The Bible relates that on the first five days of the week, God created the whole world, all the plants, animals, energy sources, and the physical environment needed by people. On the sixth day God created humans—Adam and Eve—and brought them into a world that was ready for them. There were sources of food, energy, shelter, and so forth. There was only one thing missing: a reason to live and a meaningful existence. That was created on the seventh day, which we call Shabbat. That day God created the concept of rest, that harmonious peace of mind that makes all of the stress and searching and pursuing of the first six days of the week worthwhile.

The world was created so that on six days of the week we plant, we reap, we sow, we work, we create, we hustle and bustle. But on the seventh day we stop. On that day we use our *spiritual* energies, those aspects of humanity that only humans have and that separate us from the animals. We think, we search, we interact, we socialize, we reflect, we look into ourselves, we study Torah, we draw closer to God. Shabbat creates a new dimension to our lives, it takes us out of the mundane, everyday world, involving the pursuit of material things and elevates us to a new level of spirituality and holiness.

144. Why don't we do work on Shabbat?

The Torah tells us that God doesn't want us to do work on Shabbat because we should isolate this day strictly for the spiritual and holy things in life.

There are two methods for attaining this spirituality and holiness. These methods can be defined by two words used in the Torah. The Torah tells us to "remember" the day of Shabbat and make it holy and to "guard" the day of Shabbat and make it holy.

We remember Shabbat by doing many things to make it a special day, such as lighting candles, making *Kiddush*, and singing Shabbat songs. We also have the Havdalah, Oneg Shabbat, and special elaborate meals.

We guard Shabbat by not doing certain things that would interfere with the holiness of the day. We should not make Shabbat a regular day of the week and fill it with mundane activities and experiences. The Torah prohibits thirty-nine different types of work activity, such as building, planting, cleaning, and measuring. These thirty-nine activities are mostly creative or commercial activities that people use to make a livelihood. God wanted the day of Shabbat to be free of commercial pursuits, of materialism, or of activities that make a person think that he or she is in control of the world. On six days of the week, we create, we conduct business, and we are in control. But on Shabbat we recognize that we are not the ones who actually create, control, and conduct business—it is only with the grace of God that we are able to do these things. It is God who created the world and continues the process of creating every day. On Shabbat we acknowledge this. We don't work; instead we invigorate ourselves and recharge our spiritual batteries with an extra dose of the holiness of this day.

145. Why don't some people drive cars on Shabbat?

A car is fueled by energy. To start a car, you create a fire, which burns fuel and gives the car energy. Creating fire is one of the thirty-nine activities that the Torah prohibits on Shabbat. Orthodox Jews who live a traditional lifestyle do not drive their cars on Shabbat because it involves creating a fire. In the same way, they won't even turn on their electric stoves or electric lights because it also involves creating fire. Even though these activities seem very simple and don't seem to involve a lot of work as we understand it, they are part of the creative process and so are considered impermissible on Shabbat.

146. What is *Kiddush?*

Kiddush is a special prayer that we make at the beginning of each Sabbath meal that specifically says that God made the seventh day as a holy day of rest. It is also the custom to say *Kiddush* at Friday night services. The word *kiddush* means "holy," or "to sanctify" (to set apart for a sacred purpose).

Kiddush is a specific *mitzvah,* or commandment, that we are given to sanctify Shabbat. Because Shabbat is not only a day of rest but a *holy* day of rest, we must do more than simply not work to celebrate Shabbat—we must actively raise this day above the other days. One of the ways we do this is by reciting *Kiddush.*

A beautiful thing about Judaism is that it does not teach self-denial but rather takes normal, everyday activities such as eating, and raises them to a level of holiness. By reciting *Kiddush* at the beginning of the Sabbath meal, we sanctify the meal and the family time together and make them more meaningful and special. The lovely meal and the warm feelings of family togetherness become a part of our service to God in sanctifying this day.

147. What is *Havdalah?*

The *Havdalah* service is the opposite of the *Kiddush.* The word *Havdalah* means "separation." While we recognize the start of Shabbat by reciting *Kiddush,* we recognize the conclusion of Shabbat and the return to mundane activities with the *Havdalah* service. Through this service we recognize that what we've just experienced is holy and that we are about to return to the regular, material world.

One of the most important aspects of Judaism is being able to separate and understand the difference between something that is holy and set apart and something that is of the everyday world. *Havdalah* provides us with the way to separate ourselves from Shabbat as the holy period comes to an end.

148. What is Oneg Shabbat?

Oneg Shabbat is a very happy time during Shabbat, usually used for social activities. The word *oneg* means "pleasure." Most synagogues have an Oneg Shabbat for adults and one for children, providing a healthy mix of socializing, entertaining, and religious education, giving people an opportunity to enjoy Shabbat together.

149. What is the Torah reading on Shabbat all about?

The Five Books of Moses are divided into approximately fifty-two sections, and each week a portion is read in the synagogue on Shabbat. As a means of elevating ourselves to a holy level on Shabbat, we set aside time for the study of Torah. One of the best ways to make sure we study all of the Torah is to read a different portion each week so that through the entire year, we've covered the whole Torah.

It is the custom of many Jewish families to discuss the Torah portion read that week during their festive Shabbat meals. They discuss the stories and the many lessons that can be learned from each Torah portion. Also, most Jewish schools spend some time each week studying the Torah portion for that week so that everyone can keep abreast of the Torah reading. A great rabbi once said, "It's a big *mitzvah* to be a modern Jew. To be a modern Jew means to keep up with the times. Keeping up with the times means that you're abreast each week of the Torah reading."

150. Why do we light candles on Shabbat and other holidays?

Candles bring warmth and light. The holidays and Shabbat give a sense of light and spirituality to our homes, which we represent with two lit candles. We light two candles on Shabbat because one represents the concept of *guarding* and the other of *remembering* the Sabbath. This custom was established by the sages because they felt very strongly that Shabbat should be a day of harmony and pleasantness in the home. Lit candles add brightness, warmth, and cheer, lending to the atmosphere of *shalom bayit*—peace in the home.

While lighting candles on Shabbat and other holidays, the mother of the household prays for peace and harmony in her family. Judaism believes that the mother is like the central beam in the structure of a home, and it is her duty to uphold the religious traditions and to oversee the preparations for Shabbat and holidays. By lighting the candles and saying the blessings, she brings the beauty and serenity of these special days to her family.

151. Why do we smell spices at *Havdalah?*

It is customary to smell spices at *Havdalah* to lift us out of our sadness that Shabbat is over and won't be back again for another week.

152. Why is our Shabbat on a different day from the Christian Sabbath?

Our Sabbath is based on the seventh day of creation (Saturday), which actually began on Friday night. One of the things that early Christians did to differentiate themselves from Jews was to change their Sabbath to a different day, Sunday.

153. What is the most important Jewish holiday?

Shabbat, because it comes every week, may seem as if it is not that important a holiday, but actually the Torah tells us that it is the most important holiday. It is more important than Passover and other Jewish holidays—even more important than Rosh Hashana. The only day of the year considered more holy than Shabbat is Yom Kippur, which is considered the Shabbat of Shabbats. Once a year there is even a greater Shabbat than Shabbat, and that is Yom Kippur.

Jewish History and Events

154. If God looks after the Jewish people, why have they suffered so much throughout history?

There is no question that the Jews have suffered horribly in every century throughout the history of the world. But we have always survived and have come through our troubles stronger than before. Terrible suffering is very hard for human beings to understand. We must try to accept it, and rather than try to understand why these things have happened, we must have faith in God and try to grow as we deal with the pain and suffering.

All the other ancient peoples of the world and their religions are gone, even those who conquered the Jews and destroyed our Temples. Yet even though we are so tiny in number, we are still here, having survived throughout the centuries, sometimes despite almost unbelievable odds.

God promised Abraham that we would survive as a people, and we have survived. Therefore, we must continue to have trust and faith in God and continue to live by His Torah as a shining example to the rest of the world.

155. What is an anti-Semite?

An anti-Semite is someone who hates Jews. Throughout history there have always been anti-Semites and instances of anti-Semitism. There are probably many reasons people choose to hate Jews. Often Jews have become scapegoats—blamed for others' problems—because they were seen as being different from other people. Often people don't like people who are different or whose customs they do not understand.

Jews have sometimes been seen as being more successful than other people within the societies in which they lived. That may have made people jealous of them, so often the Jews were blamed for the problems or hardships of the people in those countries. Many people didn't like the Jews because our religion did not agree with theirs. Our devotion to the Torah and its teachings and our high spirituality and standards of morality have made us targets for hate.

Since the time of the rivalry between Jacob and Esau in the Bible, the phenomenon of anti-Semitism has been with us. Most recently in the last century it was seen in Nazi Germany and in the religious persecution of Jews in Ethiopia and the Soviet Union. In the late 1980s and early 1990s, many Jews applied to leave the Soviet Union to escape from the open anti-Semitism in that country. Anti-Semitism still exists in many Arab countries today.

Jews who live in the United States, Canada, the United Kingdom, and other democracies are grateful for the opportunity to worship in peace and freedom. Jews, who know what it is to be the victims of hate, have always been leaders in the struggle for freedom, democracy, and the rights of individuals. We feel a responsibility to make sure that the rights of all people are respected, and in doing that, we know that our rights will be protected too.

156. Who were the Nazis and why did they kill so many Jews?

The Nazis were perhaps the most infamous of all anti-Semites. The Nazis rose to power in Germany during the 1930s and were led by Adolf Hitler, probably the most vicious anti-Semite of all time. The Nazis were a fascist political party that gained control of Germany and promoted the belief that German people, or Aryans, were the superior people of the world. They thought up horrible methods of ridding their country of Jews, gypsies, and other people they considered undesirable and not as good as they were.

Of all these "undesirables," Jews were the ones who were the prime targets of their viciousness, and the Nazis developed what they called their "final solution to the Jewish problem." This solution was the rounding-up and killing of all Jews. Their evil beliefs spread throughout Europe as the Nazis tried to conquer the world. They put Jews in concentration camps, first in Germany, then in other European countries. The most well known of these camps is Auschwitz. Few people survived the camps. In total, more than six million Jews were killed between the late 1930s and 1945, when World War II ended. This mass killing of our people is referred to today as the Holocaust.

The Nazis were defeated by the Allied Powers, including the United States, the United Kingdom, France, and the Soviet Union. The Nazi party is now outlawed in most countries of the world, and the very name is associated with complete evil.

There are some small groups today that hold to Nazi beliefs, but the civilized world despises them. Jewish organizations, such as the Simon Wiesenthal Center and the Anti-Defamation League of the B'nai Brith, keep track of these groups and their activities. By watching these groups carefully and using accepted laws to keep them under control, Jewish organizations work to ensure that what happened during the Holocaust will never happen again. We watch them closely to make sure that these groups will never gain too much power, and the best way to do that is to remind the world of the horrible evil that human beings are capable of, which responsible people must fight against always. The United States Holocaust Memorial Museum in Washington, D.C. is our national institution that documents, studies, and interprets Holocaust history. Also a memorial to the millions of people who died in the Holocaust, it is visited by hundreds of thousands each year.

Synagogue/Temple

157. What is a rabbi?

Rabbi literally means "teacher." The process of becoming a rabbi is an ordination, which is called *smicha*. Once the rabbi is ordained, he has a special standing because he has the ability to teach the Torah. But anyone who teaches Torah is supposed to be respected for the Torah that he knows and teaches and deserves the same respect we would give a rabbi. It is not the title that we respect but the person's knowledge of the Torah and its way of life.

In 1972 the movements outside of Orthodoxy began ordaining women as rabbis and cantors.

158. What is a cantor?

The Hebrew word for cantor is *hazan*. The cantor is the person who has been specifically trained and certified to lead the congregation in services and usually has a fine singing voice. The cantor has many duties around the synagogue including reading the Torah; chanting at weddings and, sometimes, at funerals; and leading the services at holidays, during Shabbat, and, sometimes, during the week.

159. What is a *shamash?*

The English word for *shamash* is "sexton." The *shamash's* duties are to see that the synagogue is properly serviced so that everything that takes place there runs smoothly. The *shamash* makes sure there is a *minyan,* sees that the Torahs are in readiness and prepared for the service, gives out the *aliyahs* for the Torah, and performs various other religious duties needed for the synagogue to function.

160. What is a *mohel?*

A *mohel* is another professional within the Jewish community. His job is to circumcise all the males. He is generally professionally trained and is today usually licensed with a hospital. He has learned all of the medical procedures as well as the religious procedures necessary to perform a circumcision.

161. What is a *shochet?*

A *shochet* is a person trained in the religious traditions of slaughtering animals in a kosher manner. He generally has extensive training in slaughtering and working with animals as well as knowledge of the religious requirements for preparing kosher meat.

162. What is a *mashgiach?*

A *mashgiach* is a person trained and hired by a supervising agency to see that a particular product is kosher so that the agency may certify (guarantee) the product as kosher. With the advanced technology in the food-processing industry of today, a *mashgiach* must possess knowledge of very complex processes and chemicals and procedures in preparing foods as well as all the laws of *kashrut*. This professional is very important to Jews who keep the laws of *kashrut* and want to make sure that they are doing it properly in today's society.

163. What is a synagogue?

A synagogue may also be called a *shul* (in Yiddish), a *bet haknesset* (in Hebrew), and a temple (in English). *Bet haknesset* means a place of ingathering—it is a place where Jews gather to do the most important religious functions, such as the daily and Shabbat services, the holiday services, and sometimes wedding ceremonies. In the old shtetls and ghettos, the synagogue was the only gathering place for Jews. Religious and most other activities took place there. Today it is primarily the religious gathering place for Jews.

164. What is an Aron Hakodesh?

It is the holy ark where the Torah scrolls are kept. In some synagogues other Jewish artifacts that have religious significance, such as the Haftarah scrolls, are kept there.

165. What is a bimah?

The bimah is the central place in the synagogue from which the Torah is read. The leader of the service stands at the bimah to conduct the services.

166. What is the eternal light?

There is an eternal light, or in Hebrew, a *ner tamid,* in all synagogues. Because the Torah is considered a light or a beacon that illuminates the world and the lives of people and because the concepts of the Torah are permanent and everlasting, the symbol of an eternal light that is never extinguished is placed in front of the ark in all synagogues. In addition, because each synagogue is considered a miniature Temple, a place filled with God's holy presence, we have an eternal light to remind us of the menorah in the Temple. This menorah remained lit at all times and was never extinguished.

167. Why do men and women sit separately in some synagogues?

In the time of the Temple, there were specially designated areas for men and women. The reason for this is that the Temple was a special place—the home of the Divine Presence (the spirit of God). Because it was an especially holy place, great precautions were taken so that there would be no frivolity (silliness and playfulness) or flirtatious behavior in the Temple.

We are required to really concentrate during services and think only about our devotion to God. Every synagogue is considered to have the holiness of a minor temple, so we try to keep the same level of seriousness and decorum (proper behavior) in our prayer services today as there was in the days of the Temple. For this reason, Orthodox synagogues maintain the practice of separating men and women during the prayer service so that socializing is kept to a minimum and everyone concentrates completely on the service.

168. What is a *bet hamidrash?*

A *bet hamidrash* is a little different from a *bet haknesset,* or synagogue. A synagogue is a place where people come to pray; a *bet hamidrash* is a place where people come to study. In olden days it used to be located next to the synagogue and contained many religious books. There large groups of people would study Talmud and engage in lively discussions. Today, a *bet hamidrash* can be found in the central study hall of a *yeshiva.* A synagogue can even be turned into a *bet hamidrash* during a retreat weekend when a lot of studying and discussion takes place.

169. What is a *yeshiva?*

A *yeshiva* traditionally has been a school where Torah is studied. Today a *yeshiva* is not only for Torah scholarship but is also a school where the necessary secular subjects are taught as well. Another name for *yeshiva* is Talmud Torah, which literally means the study of Torah. A Talmud Torah is generally an afternoon school that teaches Torah after regular school, unlike a *yeshiva,* which is a full-time school.

A *yeshiva* can also be an institution of higher learning, like a rabbinical college, or it may be an elementary school, which is usually called a *yeshiva katana*—a small school.

Why Do I Have to Go to Hebrew School? and Other Questions Jewish Children Ask

170. Are converts just a tad bit Christian?

No. They are 100 percent Jewish. The process of becoming a convert within Judaism is very specific. Once a person becomes a true convert, he or she is completely Jewish and tradition tells us it is as if that person stood at Mount Sinai along with all of our Jewish ancestors. A convert doesn't keep any part of his or her former religion and can serve in any role in Jewish religious life. A convert can become a rabbi, a *mohel*, or *shochet*, and can be counted in the *minyan* in even the strictest religious communities.

171. How can I be half Italian (Polish, Greek, etc.) and still be all Jewish at the same time?

Because Jews have been scattered across the world, in addition to their Jewish traditions, they have taken on the traditions and cultures of the various countries in which they have settled. We might have recipes for delicious food, as well as items of furniture, works of literature, art, music, stories, and other elements of culture inherited from our Italian (Polish, Greek, etc.) parents or grandparents. These are in addition to our rich Jewish heritage.

Just as America is a geographic melting pot, Judaism has become a cultural melting pot. During the three thousand years of the Diaspora, Judaism has become culturally enriched by the best aspects of the cultures of our host countries. That's why when Jews whose parents or grandparents have come from many different places get together, we are such an exciting, varied, and interesting group. We have our Jewish traditions in common, and we also have our varied ethnic backgrounds to spice things up.

172. If my grandparents came from Russia, am I part Russian?

No. You are an American (Canadian, Israeli, etc.) Jew with a Russian flavor.

173. What do people mean when they refer to Ashkenazic and Sephardic Jews?

Ashkenazic Jews are descendants of Jews from Central and Eastern European countries, such as Germany, Poland, Russia, and France. Sephardic Jews are descendants of Jews from Spain, Portugal, Egypt, Turkey, and other Mediterranean countries. Many Jews in South American countries are also of Sephardic descent.

If you would like to know if you are an Ashkenazic or a Sephardic Jew, find out where your grandparents or great-grandparents came from.

174. What is Yiddish?

Yiddish has been the common language of Ashkenazic Jews; it has developed over the last thousand years. It is a mixture of many different languages and dialects. It is usually written using the Hebrew alphabet. In each country where Jews have lived and spoken Yiddish, many new words and variations of the native language were mixed into the local Yiddish dialect. Thus modern Yiddish has become a colorful language with a vocabulary drawn from Russian, German, Hebrew, Polish, Hungarian, and other languages.

Nevertheless Yiddish has remained a uniquely Jewish language. Much has been written in Yiddish, including religious books, poetry, novels, plays, and music. Although Yiddish is not as popular today as it once was, there are many societies and cultural groups that continue to promote its use.

Many Yiddish words have found their way into the English language, such as *shtick, chutzpah, oy, shlep,* and hundreds of other colorful terms.

A great source of Yiddish words, stories, and jokes is *The Joys of Yiddish* by Leo Rosten.

175. What is Ladino?

Ladino is a Sephardic language spoken and written by Jews from Sephardic lands, mainly from the fifteenth through nineteenth centuries. It is a combination of Hebrew, Arabic, Greek, Aramaic, Turkish, and other Mediterranean languages. It was primarily a religious language. Many original works and translations of religious books were written in Ladino so that they would be read by a large number of Sephardic Jews.

176. Does our tradition discourage dating non-Jews?

Yes. For five thousand years we as a people have striven to retain our Jewish identities. We have survived and overcome a great deal. Our traditions are rich and full and we have contributed much to humanity. If we practice Judaism and fill our lives with it, we will make the world a better place for ourselves and everyone else in it. That is our duty and our responsibility—that's the way we were born. It is incumbent on us to learn more about our Judaism, to appreciate Judaism more, to have the desire to continue our religion, and to pass it on to future generations of Jews.

We were put in this world to do our job as Jews and to continue the Jewish people. We can do that only if we find a mate within Judaism.

Therefore, when it comes to the point in our lives when we're ready to date (and that becomes a stepping-stone to finding a mate), Judaism believes that we must do our utmost to see to it that we seek out a Jewish mate. The best way to do this is to date other Jews. If we intermarry, all that we treasure can become lost.

177. Are most people in the world Jewish?

No. Quite the contrary. Numerically, Jews are only a tiny

minority of the world population. In fact, it is estimated that out of the approximately five billion people in the world, only seventeen million or so are Jewish. That makes the world Jewish population only 0.33 percent of the world population.

It is quite extraordinary that Jews make such an impact in the world and yet are so few in number compared with other peoples. The famous American author, essayist, and humorist Mark Twain wrote a long article about the Jews, which was published in 1898. This is how the article concluded:

If the statistics are right, the Jews constitute but *one percent* of the human race. It suggests a nebulous dim puff of star dust lost in the blaze of the Milky Way. Properly the Jew ought hardly to be heard of; but he is heard of, has always been heard of. He is as prominent on the planet as any other people, and his commercial importance is extravagantly out of proportion to the smallness of his bulk. His contributions to the world's list of great names in literature, science, art, music, finance, medicine, and abstruse learning are also way out of proportion to the weakness of his numbers. He has made a marvelous fight in this world, in all the ages; and has done it with his hands tied behind him. He could be vain of himself, and be excused for it. The Egyptian, the Babylonian, and the Persian rose, filled the planet with sound and splendor, then faded to dreamstuff and passed away; the Greek and the Roman followed, and made a vast noise, and they are gone; other peoples have sprung up and held their torch high for a time, but it burned out, and they sit in twilight now, or have vanished. The Jew saw them all, beat them all, and is now what he always was, exhibiting no decadence, no infirmities of age, no weakening of his parts, no slowing of his energies, no dulling of his alert and aggressive mind. All things are mortal but the Jew; all other forces pass, but he remains. What is the secret of his immortality?

178. What does it mean when someone calls you a JAP?
JAP is a snide, ethnic slur, an insult. It pokes fun at what some people believe is a Jewish shortcoming—the notion that Jewish girls are spoiled. It's a stereotype, and just as we should not stereotype any ethnic group or generalize about it or contribute to perceptions that are unfair and often incorrect, we certainly shouldn't do it to each other. We should not encourage misconceptions, we should avoid stereotyping ourselves or others, and we should never insult our own people by using this term or any other slur.

179. What is a Gentile?
A Gentile is someone who is not Jewish.

180. Why do some people write "G–D"?
Because the name of God is considered holy in any language in which it is written, a letter or document that contains the name of God will take on that holiness. Therefore, it has become the tradition among many people not to spell out the full name of God so that a paper that has God's name on it can be discarded or defaced in any manner one chooses.

181. How should people dispose of papers and books containing God's name?

All holy items used for religious purposes, such as *tefillin*, prayer books, *mezuzot*, and Bibles are to be treated with great respect, even when they are old and worn out. Because of the holiness attached to them, they must be disposed of in a special, respectful way. This is done by burying them, returning them to nature in the same way that bodies are buried and returned to nature. They are in a sense recycled. Synagogues have a special place where these items are temporarily stored, and every Jewish cemetery has a special area called a *genizah* where these items are eventually buried.

182. Why do I have to go to Hebrew School?

A lot of kids think Hebrew School is a waste of their time. Maybe you do, too. Often it comes after a long day of regular school. Maybe there is time for a quick snack before rushing off to Hebrew School, maybe there is not. Maybe other friends of yours also go to Hebrew School, and maybe some of your Jewish friends don't. Maybe there is a lot of homework from regular school on Hebrew School nights. Maybe you have a sports or party conflict, and your parents insist that Hebrew School comes first. And although Hebrew School is sometimes interesting and fun, sometimes it really isn't. Maybe, like Rachel, Mitchel, Steven, and some of their friends, you also ask your parents, "Why do I have to go to Hebrew School?"

The answer is "Because . . ."

- Because we love you and want you to know as much about being Jewish as you possibly can
- Because we parents often don't know as much as we possibly could about being Jewish and can't give you all the right answers
- Because at Hebrew School you get to learn and socialize with other Jewish children, just like yourself (who may sometimes wonder why they have to go, too)
- Because one of the most important things the Torah expects of parents is that they teach their children Torah—and if we are unable to do that, we are obligated to find someone who can do it for us
- Because Judaism has a rich and full heritage older than five thousand years, with lots to learn about, enjoy, and appreciate, and Hebrew School is a great place to be introduced to it
- Because if you didn't go and later found out all that you had missed, you'd probably be mad at your parents
- Because Judaism is precious and beautiful and important and your parents want you to share in it and be connected to it
- Because whatever career or role in life you pursue, the knowledge and information you gain in Hebrew School will enrich you in ways you cannot even imagine
- Because this book can't possibly answer all the questions you might have about Judaism, Hebrew School is the place to seek out more information
- Because Judaism is more than just a religion—it is a way of life
- Because all of Judaism is based on scholarship and study.

If we spent our whole lives studying Torah, we still wouldn't know everything there is to know about living our lives the way God wants us to live them

- Because at Hebrew School you learn to read Hebrew so that you can understand what is going on at services
- Because at Hebrew School you learn all you need to know to fully participate in your bar or bat mitzvah ceremony
- Because to be a good Jew you must first be a knowledgeable Jew
- Because sometimes we parents know what is really best for you, and you just have to trust us (in the same way that we all have to trust that God knows what is best for us, even when we don't understand why)
- Because sometimes, as children, you don't yet have the ability to appreciate really good things and will realize how good those things truly are only when you get older (Do most kids like vegetables all the time? Don't most adults?)
- Because Hebrew School is just as important as, and in some ways may be more important than, public school.
- Because you are so fortunate that there is the State of Israel in your lifetime and going to Hebrew School is a great way to strengthen your connection to Israel and to the Israelis—by learning the history, songs, and stories of our homeland and its people
- Because, unlike those Jewish children in some countries who are not allowed to learn and practice Judaism, you are lucky enough to live in freedom with the right to study your religion openly
- Because although Judaism has survived all kinds of per-

secution and disasters throughout the ages, it cannot survive indifference and neglect by its own people

- Because the only way for you to continue the unbroken chain of Judaism is to study it, know it, and pass it along to your children. You are a precious link in this chain, which stretches back through generations, and while you may add to it, you should not break it

That way, someday years from now when your children ask you, "Why do I have to go to Hebrew School?" you can smile at them very knowingly and answer, "Because."

Glossary

AGGADAH. The moral, ethical, and philosophical meanings behind the words of the Bible.

ALIYAH. The honor of being called to the Torah.

ABRAHAM. The first Jew, the father of the Jewish people.

AMIDAH. *See* Shmoneh Esrei.

ARON HAKODESH. The holy ark where the Torah scrolls are kept.

ASHKENAZIM. Jews whose ancestors are from Eastern and Central European countries.

AVODAH. Hebrew word meaning "service to God."

BAR AND BAT MITZVAH. The age of responsibility, according to Jewish law. Literally means "son (or daughter) of the commandments." Commonly used to describe the ceremony at which a boy or girl publicly recognizes his or her coming of age as an adult Jew.

BEMIDBAR. Hebrew for "Numbers," the fourth book of the Bible.

BERESHIT. Hebrew for "Genesis," the first book of the Bible.

BET HAKNESSET. Hebrew for "synagogue."

BET HAMIDRASH. A place where people come to study.

BIMAH. Central place in the synagogue from which the Torah is read.

BRIT MILAH (BRIS). The Covenant between God and Abraham; also refers to the ceremony of circumcision.

CHAF. Hebrew letter with the gutteral *kh* sound.

CHAI. Hebrew for "life"; also the number eighteen.

CHET. Hebrew letter with the gutteral *kh* sound.

CHUMASH. Hebrew for "five." Another name for the Five Books of Moses.

CHUPPAH. The canopy beneath which Jewish marriages are performed.

DEVARIM. Hebrew for "Deuteronomy," the fifth book of the Bible.

DIASPORA. A term that refers to the Jewish population living outside of Israel, dating from the Babylonian exile.

DREIDEL. The four-sided top played with during Hanukkah.

EREV. Evening, which begins the Jewish day.

ETROG. A citrus fruit, significant in the celebration of Sukkot.

FIVE BOOKS OF MOSES. The first five of the twenty-four books of the Bible.

FLEISHIG. Meat foods.

GEMARA. Another name for the Talmud; the commentary on the Mishnah.

GENIZAH. The permanent burial place for used holy books and writings.

GENTILE. A non-Jew.

GIMEL. Hebrew letter with the *g* sound.

HAFTARAH. The portion of the Books of the Prophets that is read in the synagogue each week.

HAGGADAH. The book used during the Passover Seder, which contains the songs, prayers, and story of the flight from Egypt.

HAMETZ. The category of foods not permitted to be eaten during Passover. These include grains and their by-products, such as leavened bread and grain alcohol.

HALAKAH. The laws of the Bible; Jewish law.

HANUKKIYAH. The nine-branched candelabrum lit during Hanukkah.

HASIDIM. A sect of Orthodox Jews who practice an emotional, intense form of Judaism.

HAVDALAH. The special prayer said at the end of Shabbat to separate the holiness of Shabbat from the regular work week.

HAY. Hebrew letter with the *h* sound.

HAZAN. A cantor.

HILLEL. The great Jewish scholar who set the Jewish calendar. He was first to specify the Golden Rule (Do not do to your neighbor what is hateful to yourself).

KADDISH. A prayer of praise to God, which is said in public by a mourner on behalf of the community.

KASHRUT. The dietary laws governing the preparation procedures for kosher food and the guidelines for eating it.

KETUVIM. Writings and Psalms, part of the twenty-four books of the Bible.

KETUBAH. The Jewish marriage contract, which spells out the duties of a husband and a wife to each other.

KIDDUSH. The special prayer that sets apart the Sabbath as a holy day of rest.

KIPPAH. A skullcap worn as a head covering, also called a yarmulke.

KOHEN, KOHANIM (PLURAL). A priest of the Temple in Jerusalem.

KOHEN GADOL. The high priest who conducted services in the Temple on Yom Kippur; he was the only one allowed into the Holy of Holies.

KOTEL. Hebrew name for the Western Wall in Jerusalem.

LADINO. A Sephardic language used mainly from the fifteenth through nineteenth centuries.

LAG. Hebrew word which is the numerical equivalent of thirty-three.

LATKES. Potato pancakes fried in oil; a traditional Hanukkah dish.

LEVI, LEVITES (PLURAL). A Jew who is a descendant of Jacob's son Levi and his tribe.

L'SHANA TOVA TIKATEVU. Traditional Rosh Hashana greeting, which means "May you be inscribed for a good year."

LUBAVITCH. One of the many groups of Hasidic Jews.

LULAV. A palm branch, significant in the celebration of Sukkot.

MACHZOR. The holiday prayer book.

MASHGIACH. A person trained and hired by a supervising agency to see that a particular product is kosher.

MASHIACH. The anointed one; the Messiah.

MEGILLAH. Commonly used to refer to the Book of Esther, which contains the story of Purim.

MENORAH. The seven-branched candelabrum used in the Temple.

MEZUZAH. A little parchment scroll bearing two of the most important passages from the Torah, kept inside a decorative case that is placed on the doorposts of Jewish homes.

MILCHIG. Dairy foods.

MINHAG. A local custom (as opposed to a law), practiced in some places but not others.

MINYAN. A traditional quorum of ten Jewish men over bar mitzvah age.

MISHLOACH MANOT. Another way of saying *shalach monos,* which means sending presents on Purim.

MISHNAH. An encyclopedia of Jewish laws based on the Bible; part of the Talmud.

MITZVAH, MITZVOT (PLURAL). Commandment; also used to refer to a good deed.

MOHEL. A person professionally trained to perform circumcision.

MOSES MAIMONIDES. A great teacher, rabbi, writer, physician, and adviser to the sultan of Egypt. He lived eight hundred years ago.

NER TAMID. The eternal light, which burns continuously in all synagogues.

NES GADOL HAYAH PO. "A great miracle happened here," written on dreidels in Israel, in reference to Hanukkah.

NES GADOL HAYAH SHAM. "A great miracle happened there," written on dreidels outside of Israel, in reference to Hanukkah.

NESHAMA. Soul.

NIVIIM. The Books of the Prophets, part of twenty-four books of the Bible.

NUN. Hebrew letter with the *n* sound.

OMER. The period of time between Passover and Shavuot.

PAREVE. Foods that are neither *milchig* (dairy) nor *fleishig* (meat).

PAY. Hebrew letter with a *p* sound.

PUSHKE. A coin box used for the giving of charity.

RABBI AKIVA. A famous Jewish scholar.

REBBE. Teacher; Yiddish for rabbi.

SANHEDRIN. The seventy elders of the Jews who presided over the government during the days of the Temple.

SARAH. The wife of Abraham; the first matriarch of the Jewish people.

SATAN. The evil force.

SCHACH. The greenery covering a *sukkah*.

SEDER. Hebrew for "order," the celebratory Passover service, which includes a festive meal.

SEPHARDIM. Jews whose ancestors came from Mediterranean countries.

SEUDAH. A festive meal.

SHEMOT. Hebrew for "Exodus," the second book of the Bible.

SHEVAH BERAKHOT. The seven special blessings celebrating a marriage.

SHALACH MONOS. Another way of saying *mishloach manot*, which means "sending presents" on Purim.

SHAMASH. Sexton.

SHAMUS. A temporary storage place for disposing of used holy books and writings.

SHEKEL. An Israeli coin.

SHALOM BAYIT. Hebrew for "peace in the home."

SHIN. Hebrew letter with the *sh* sound.

SH'MA. The most fundamental Jewish prayer.

SHMONEH ESREI. A fundamental Jewish prayer composed of eighteen essential blessings, which we request from God.

SHOCHET. A person trained in the religious traditions of slaughtering animals in a kosher manner.

SHOFAR. A ram's horn blown during services on the High Holidays of Rosh Hashana and Yom Kippur.

SHUL. A synagogue.

SHULCHAN ARUCH. The main body of codification (listing) of Jewish law, compiled by Rabbi Joseph Karo.

SIDDUR. The Shabbat and weekday prayer book.

SOFER. A Hebrew scribe.

SPIEL. A play presented during Purim.

SUKKAH. A booth, which is a temporary structure, used to celebrate Sukkot.

TAV. Hebrew letter with the *t* sound.

TALLIT. A four-cornered prayer shawl with *tzitzit* at each corner.

TALMUD. The main body of Jewish religious writings, including law, history, philosophy, moral teachings, and legends.

TANACH. A Hebrew word for the Bible. *Tanach* is an acronym made up of three Hebrew letters: *tav* for Torah, *nun* for *Niviim,* and *chaf* for *Ketuvim.*

TASHLICH. Hebrew for "to send." The custom of offering a prayer near a body of running water and tossing crumbs from our pockets into the water to symbolize the cleansing of our sins. This takes place between Rosh Hashana and Yom Kippur.

TEFILLIN. Two small boxes with leather straps attached to them, containing passages from the Bible. They are worn during weekday morning prayer services.

TORAH. In the broadest sense, refers to any form of Jewish religious teaching. Generally refers to the first five books of the Bible, called the Five Books of Moses.

TESHUVAH. Repentance.

TZEDAKAH. Literally means "righteousness." Used to refer to charity.

TZITZIT. The white-and-blue fringe worn at each corner of a *tallit.*

VAYIKRA. Hebrew for "Leviticus," the third book of the Bible.

VILNA GAON. A great rabbi and Talmudic scholar who lived in the 1700s.

YAHRZEIT. The yearly anniversary of someone's death, figured according to the Jewish calendar.

YARMULKE. A skullcap worn as a head covering; also called a *kippah*.

YESHIVA, YESHIVOT (PLURAL). A Jewish religious school.

YETZER HARAH. The evil inclination.

YIDDISH. The common language of Ashkenazic Jews, a mixture of many different languages and dialects, written in the Hebrew alphabet.

YISRAEL. A Jew who is neither a Kohen nor a Levi.

YIZKOR. Hebrew for "to remember." A special prayer or service said by relatives in memory of a loved one who has died.

YOM HA ATZMA'UT. Israel Independence Day.

YOM HASHOAH. Holocaust Remembrance Day.

YOM HAZIKARON. Memorial Day for fallen Israeli soldiers.

YOM YERUSHALAYIM. Modern holiday commemorating the 1967 reunification of the city of Jerusalem.

YOD. Hebrew letter with the y sound.

Index

Index

Day of Judgment, 74

Death

  reward for righteousness and
    punishment for evil after, 19

  where we go after we die, 19

Deuteronomy (*Devarim*), 31

Diaspora, 40, 83

Dreidel, game of, 76–77

Eternal light, 106

Etrog, 91

Exodus (*Shemot*), 30, 32

Five Books of Moses, 27, 30–31

Forefathers and foremothers, 36

Genesis (*Bereshit*), 30, 36

Gentile, 114

Glossary, 119–26

God

  all-knowingness of, 5

  animals getting hit by cars and,
    2

  bad people and, 3–4

  disposing of papers and books
    containing God's name, 115

  feelings of, 4

  "G–D" for, 114

  God's expectations of Jews, 5

  origin and existence of, 5

  physical appearance of, 1

  sickness and suffering and, 2–3

  ways of talking to us, 1–2

Haftarah, 28–29

Haggadah, 80

Halakah, 33, 57

Haman, 83–85

Hanukkah

  eating latkes on, 77

  lighting candles on, 74–75

  meaning of, 75–76

  relationship to Christmas, 77

Hasidim, 62–63

Havdalah, 95–96

  smelling spices at, 98

Heaven, bad people in, 20

Hebrew

  learning, 49

  praying together in, 49

Hebrew calendar, months of, 67

Hebrew School, 115–18

High Holidays, 69–70

Hillel, 82–83

Hitler, Adolf, 84, 101

Holidays

Index

Index

Index

About the Authors

RABBI E. B. FREEDMAN is the director of the Jewish Hospice and Chaplaincy Network, counseling hundreds of families of all backgrounds. He was previously the director of Yeshivath Beth Yehudah, a Hebrew and secular school attended by more than six hundred children between the ages of four and eighteen—the same school he attended as a child. He was graduated from Beth Medrosh Govoha in Lakewood, New Jersey, the largest and most prominent Orthodox rabbinical seminary in the United States. He was head counselor at a number of Jewish summer camps and was the director of the Kollel Institute, a center of advanced Jewish education in Michigan, where he lives with his wife. They have seven children and three grandchildren.

JAN GREENBERG is an award-winning author whose work has appeared on the *New York Times* bestseller list and has been translated into several languages. She has a bachelor of arts degree from the University of Illinois and has recently completed her twenty-fifth novel. She is a member of Temple Israel, a Reform congregation, and is an active supporter of

Jewish causes. She and her husband are parents of a lovely grown daughter. They live in Michigan with their Yorkshire terrier Scamper.

KAREN A. KATZ is a writer of fiction and nonfiction and a professional artist. She and her husband, parents of two grown sons, live in Michigan. She has a bachelor's degree from Wayne State University and is a veteran journalist and public-relations specialist. A member of Congregation Shaarey Zedek, a Conservative synagogue, she sits on the board of trustees and served as Sisterhood president. She has also been active for many years in Zionist causes.